THE LIBRARY OF HOLOCAUST TESTIMONIES

No Place to Run

The Library of Holocaust Testimonies

Editors: Antony Polonsky, Martin Gilbert CBE, Aubrey Newman,
Raphael F. Scharf, Ben Helfgott MBE

Under the auspices of the Yad Vashem Committee of the Board of
Deputies of British Jews and the Centre for Holocaust Studies,
University of Leicester

My Lost World by Sara Rosen
From Dachau to Dunkirk by Fred Pelican
Breathe Deeply, My Son by Henry Wermuth
My Private War by Jacob Gerstenfeld-Maltiel
A Cat Called Adolf by Trude Levi
An End to Childhood by Miriam Akavia
A Child Alone by Martha Blend
The Children Accuse by Maria Hochberg-Marianska and Noe Gruss
I Light a Candle by Gena Turgel
My Heart in a Suitcase by Anne L. Fox
Memoirs from Occupied Warsaw, 1942–1945
by Helena Szereszewska
Have You Seen My Little Sister?
by Janina Fischler-Martinho
Surviving the Nazis, Exile and Siberia by Edith Sekules
Out of the Ghetto by Jack Klajman with Ed Klajman
From Thessaloniki to Auschwitz and Back 1926–1996
by Erika Myriam Kounio Amariglio
Translated by Theresa Sundt
I Was No. 20832 at Auschwitz by Eva Tichauer
Translated by Colette Lévy and Nicki Rensten
My Child is Back! by Ursula Pawel
Wartime Experiences in Lithuania by Rivka Lozansky Bogomolnaya
Translated by Miriam Beckerman
Who Are You, Mr Grymek? by Natan Gross
A Life Sentence of Memories by Issy Hahn, Foreword by Theo Richmond
An Englishman in Auschwitz by Leon Greenman
For Love of Life by Leah Iglinsky-Goodman
No Place to Run: The Story of David Gilbert
by Tim Shortridge and Michael D. Frounfelter
A Little House on Mount Carmel by Alexandre Blumstein
From Germany to England Via the Kindertransports by Peter Prager
By a Twist of History: The Three Lives of a Polish Jew by Mietek Sieradzki
The Jews of Poznań by Zbigniew Pakula
Lessons in Fear by Henryk Vogler

No Place to Run

A True Story

As told by

David Gilbert

Written by Tim Shortridge and
Michael D. Frounfelter

VALLENTINE MITCHELL
LONDON • PORTLAND, OR

First Published in 2002 in Great Britain by
VALLENTINE MITCHELL
Crown House, 47 Chase Side
Southgate, London N14 5BP

and in the United States of America by
VALLENTINE MITCHELL
c/o ISBS, 5824 N. E. Hassalo Street
Portland, Oregon 97213-3644

Website: http://www.vmbooks.com

British Library Cataloguing in Publication Data

Shortridge, Tim
    No place to run: a true story as told by David (Götzel)
Gilbert. – (The library of Holocaust testimonies)
1. Gilbert, David 2. Jews – Poland 3. Holocaust, Jewish
(1939–1945) – Personal narratives, Polish
I. Title II. Frounfelter, Michael D.
940.5'318'09438'092

ISBN 0-8530-3422-2
ISSN 1363-3759

Library of Congress Cataloguing-in-Publication Data

Gilbert, David (David Götzel).
    No place to run: a true story/as told by David (Götzel) Gilbert; written by Tim
Shortridge and Michael D. Frounfelter.
    p. cm. – (The library of Holocaust testimonies, ISSN 1363–3759)
    ISBN 0-8530-3422-2 (pbk.)
    1. Gilbert, David. 2. Jews–Poland–Biography. 3. Holocaust, Jewish
(1939–1945)–Personal narratives. 4. Poland–Biography. I. Shortridge, Tim. II.
Frounfelter, Michael D. III. Title. iv. Series.

DS135.P63 G53555 2001
940.53'18'092–dc21
[B]
                                                                        2001044570

Typeset in 10.75/14 Palatino by Cambridge Photosetting Services
Printed in & bound by MPG Books Ltd, Bodmin, Cornwall.

Dedicated to the New Life Club of San Diego

Contents

List of Illustrations

The Library of Holocaust Testimonies

It is greatly to the credit of Frank Cass that this series of survivors' testimonies is being published in Britain. The need for such a series has long been apparent here, where many survivors made their homes.

Since the end of the War in 1945 the terrible events of the Nazi destruction of European Jewry have cast a pall over our time. Six million Jews were murdered within a short period; the few survivors have had to carry in their memories whatever remains of the knowledge of Jewish life in more than a dozen countries, in several thousand towns, in tens of thousands of villages, and in innumerable families. The precious gift of recollection has been the sole memorial for millions of people whose lives were suddenly and brutally cut off.

For many years, individual survivors have published their testimonies. But many more have been reluctant to do so, often because they could not believe that they would find a publisher for their efforts.

In my own work over the past two decades, I have been approached by many survivors who had set down their memories in writing, but who did not know how to have them published. I realized what a considerable emotional strain the writing down of such hellish memories had been. I also realized, as I read many dozens of such accounts, how important each account was, in its own way, in recounting aspects of the story that had not been told before, and adding to our understanding of the wide range of human suffering, struggle and aspiration.

With so many people and so many places involved, including many hundreds of camps, it was inevitable that the historians and students of the Holocaust should find it difficult at times to grasp the scale and range of the events. The publication of memoirs is therefore an indispensable part of the extension of knowledge, and of public awareness of the crimes that had been committed against a whole people.

Martin Gilbert
Merton College, Oxford

A Note to the Reader

You've heard the Holocaust statistics. Millions of people slaughtered. And yet, as horrible as those statistics are, I've noticed at speaking engagements that a firsthand account from one survivor can have a greater impact with listeners. A survivor's story personalizes those numbers.

For those of us who struggled through that dark time, the Holocaust was personal. The Nazis wanted to kill ME. They wanted to kill MY family. I am 88 years old, and I don't have much time left to tell my story. So I have put it down on paper. As you read it, remember that it is only one story. There are millions of others. And this story is certainly not the most important: it just happens to be mine.

Tim Shortridge, Michael D. Frounfelter and I attempted to reconstruct my story so that you can experience what it was like to be a Jew in Nazi-occupied Europe. This memoir is based on my best recollection of the events, along with corroborating research, to help get the dates and details right. There are, however, some necessary limitations on the literal 'truthfulness' of this writing. Although I've lost contact with most of the people within these pages, many of them, I hope, still enjoy happy and healthy lives. To protect their privacy, we changed their names. In addition, we occasionally omitted or altered insignificant events and details that were unimportant to the story. This resulted in some minor characters being a composite of two or more people and some minor events being slightly altered. The

xiii

core of the story, however, is accurate.

We wrote the story in simple English to make it easy to read. During the events described, of course, Polish and German were spoken. Whenever the language being used is important, we mention or indicate it.

To depict the events my wife experienced in my absence, and her frame of mind during that time, we relied heavily on her personal memoirs and the many discussions I had with her over the years since.

Finally, my memory of this period is not perfect. We had to reinvent much of the dialogue based on my recollection. Our intention was to capture the flavour of the events and conversations that took place. If we succeeded, then I believe you will come to understand what living in those times was like. I believe too that with that understanding, you'll want to ensure that nothing such as this ever happens again.

David Gilbert (Götzel)
September 2001

1 *Invasion*

Friday, 1 September 1939. As dawn begins to brighten our bedroom window, my wife Sophie gently shakes my arm. 'David, are you awake?'

'Ja.' Her hand feels warm against my skin.

'Do you hear that?' she whispers.

There is a deep resonating vibration. It is distant, but growing steadily louder, closer. I place my hand on hers. 'I've been listening to it for a while.'

'They don't sound Polish.'

Day and night for months now, Polish aircraft have been flying manoeuvres over the Warsaw countryside. In our cottage, just outside Warsaw, we had grown accustomed to them. In the evenings, the distant drone often lulls me to sleep. But Sophie is right, this isn't the sound of Polish aircraft. This sound is deeper, stronger, louder. It's starting to rattle the windows.

I climb out of bed. 'Wait here.' As I hurry through the cottage, the rumbling grows stronger. My whole body quivers from the onslaught. The fear I have suppressed for years rises to the surface. Don't be the Germans. Not yet. Not now!

Outside, the bright morning sky ripples black. Waves of aircraft, like geese migrating from as far west as I can see, fly toward me in V formations. The first wave thunders overhead. Groups of twin-engine planes fly high above scattered clouds, their wing-tips dissolving into the clouds, then reappearing. Groups of single-engine planes fly lower. Black crosses are

1

painted on the undersides of their wings. They are definitely not Polish.

The roar pulses in my ears, reverberates in my chest. Then the next wave thunders over. Three smaller planes swoop down over a grove of beeches, their underbellies skimming the tree-tops. They scream past me on a direct line to Warsaw. Painted prominently on their tails are black swastikas.

Anguish rips through me. I cover my face and cry out, 'No!' I feel dizzy and my breath comes in short gasps. I try to steady myself. I am such a fool! Stupid, stupid fool! What have I done? Stayed in Poland too long. I never meant to but since Micki's birth, money has been short. It doesn't matter. The question is, what are we going to do now?

I shake with fear. My mind races. We have some food in the cottage, and a little in our apartment in Mokotow, but not enough.

Both my mind and body scream: get away! RUN! But where? The Germans are probably marching towards us from the west and south. The Baltic Sea to the north offers no refuge. And east is Stalin, a dictator I trust less than Hitler. For all I know, the Russians might be attacking from that direction. We could be surrounded by fighting.

Through the living room window, I see Sophie sitting on the edge of the couch. Her short brown hair sticks out at odd angles. I can see the fear in her eyes, magnified by her thick glasses. She bounces our daughter Micki, who's not yet two years old, on her knee. Wanda, our nanny, fidgets on the couch beside them. Micki tugs on Wanda's blonde braid.

The roar of aircraft engulfs us all. It is my fault that we are trapped here, surrounded by war. Now what? I walk back inside.

'Germans?' Sophie yells above the noise. I nod.

'The phone's not working,' Wanda says.

'We should never have come here!' Sophie yells, rocking back and forth on the couch.

I kneel before her, taking her hands in mine. 'I'm sorry, Sophie. It's all my fault. Please forgive me.'

'It's not your fault,' she says, shaking her head.

'We shouldn't be here. I should have applied for emigration sooner, should have tried harder . . . Should have done something. And now . . .'

'It's not your fault,' she whispers.

Micki nestles against my chest. My throat tightens. It *is* my fault. Tears spill down Sophie's cheeks. I wipe them away. 'I think everything will be all right,' I say, trying hard to believe it. 'First, let's find out what's going on. Wanda, please turn on the radio.'

Wanda crosses the living room to where the radio sits on the dining table. She turns it on, but I can't hear it above the planes. Micki starts coughing. Phlegm rattles in her chest. She's still recovering from whooping cough. The doctor said a stay in the country would be good for her. That's why we rented this cottage. Sophie pats her back.

'Once I know what's happening,' I say, 'I'll figure out the best place to go.' She looks away, bites her lower lip. 'Everything's going to be all right, *Häschen*.' (*Häschen* is German for my little bunny. It always makes her smile. It works this time, too.) She nods her agreement.

For two hours, aircraft thunder over our heads before the sky is finally quiet. Too afraid to go outside, we sit around the table in the dining area of the living room. I twist the radio knob in search of news. There must be useful information out there somewhere, a radio signal not filled with static, German propaganda, or marching music. So far, I have only been able to get the local stations, and they know very little.

'Wait,' I say, holding up my hand. 'It's the BBC.'

A soft English voice speaks, 'At daybreak this morning, the German Army . . .' Loud static interrupts. A moment later, Hitler's voice bellows forth in German, 'Poland cannot attack Germany without retaliation. At this moment, our planes are

3

flying over Poland and our army is marching toward Warsaw. We shall not rest before occupying all of Poland.'

I had heard this speech earlier. I snap off the radio, resisting the urge to smash it on the floor. 'They're boosting their radio signals, trying to drown out all other stations, cut us off from the rest of the world.' I stand and pace across the living room. 'If only I could find out what's going on.'

'What did he say?' Wanda asks. She is not fluent in German.

'Lies,' I say. 'He claims Polish soldiers attacked a German radio station. Why would they do that? They know he's been looking for an excuse to start a war.'

Sophie crushes out her cigarette in the ashtray by the radio. 'I guess he found one.'

Silence fills the room. My ears hum from the earlier noise. I look at Sophie and see terror on her face. I feel it, too. It's seeping into the cottage like the fog that seeped between the spruce trees of the Black Forest where I grew up and where I was living when the last war ended. I was only five years old then, but I remember the terror clearly.

I walk to the window and look up at the azure sky. A lone sparrow lands on the front gate. It twitches and flutters. Sophie joins me. 'What are we going to do?' She wraps her arms around me, rests her head on my back. I pull her arms tighter around me and close my eyes. What are we going to do? That is the question, isn't it? What can we do? If only I knew what was going on. But without phones or reliable radio stations . . . I wonder if I could learn anything in town?

I look back out the window. The sparrow is gone, the sky empty. I turn to Sophie. 'I think I'll walk into town, buy some food. Then we'll wait and see what happens over the weekend.'

I approach Skolimow just after eleven. My legs ache from the hurried, five-kilometre walk. The sun beats hot against my back. Sweat soaks my face and neck. At the railroad station, people jam along the tracks, jostling to board the next train to Warsaw.

Despite the heat, the windows and shutters of the town's red-brick houses are closed. About 500 people – a third of the town's residents – crowd the main street. They scurry over the cobble-stones like fieldmice fleeing a fire.

I enter the small wooden building of the post office. The people inside the tiny room refuse to organize themselves into queues: they are unwilling to wait their turn. I elbow my way toward one of the two windows. An elderly woman bursts through the doorway. 'The army has collapsed! The Germans are on the outskirts of Warsaw.'

'Rubbish,' replies a raspy male voice. 'We're too well equipped. I hear we're holding the lines near the border.'

'It's true!' the woman screams. 'We have to get away!'

'Go and spread your rumours somewhere else,' the man says. He turns to the young woman next to him. 'What are you doing? I'm next.' The elderly woman rushes back outside. The door slams behind her.

'Who can know what's true?' I say to the clerk behind the window. He stares at me with bloodshot eyes. I request half the money in our postal savings account. He starts counting and then stops. 'That's not right,' he mumbles, and starts again. It takes him three tries to get it right.

Down the street from the post office I find a carriage for hire. The driver, a burly man with a scruffy beard, demands twice the usual rate.

The crowd inside the general store is well-behaved. The owners, 50-year-old twin brothers, stand behind the counter in matching plaid shirts. One handles customers. The other cradles a shotgun. I walk among the mostly barren shelves and collect some sugar, salt, sardines and a few canned goods. Not much here. I stand in line behind a well-dressed woman in her mid-thirties – probably a visitor to the town's spa.

She speaks to the brother holding the shotgun, 'I heard that England and France invaded Germany from the west. The Americans are expected to join them soon.'

'That's not what I heard,' says a toothless old woman standing behind me. There are deep furrows in the blotchy skin of her face. 'I heard we're about to surrender. Everyone with any sense is fleeing to Russia.'

'Rumours,' I say to the owner. 'Aren't you tired of rumours?'

He props his shotgun on his hip. 'You sound German.'

My chest tightens. I hadn't considered how the townspeople might react to my accent. 'I was born in Germany,' I say quickly, 'but I've lived in Warsaw for the past four years.' I drop my groceries on the counter and fumble for my passport. 'My father emigrated to Germany before I was born, but never became a citizen. See, my passport is Polish. My wife and I are renting Piotr Wasilewski's cottage just outside town.'

My hands shake as the brothers look at my passport, then each other. The one holding the shotgun says, 'On your way.'

'Please, allow me to buy my groceries.' He nods.

Outside, I load my purchases into the bottom of the carriage. The driver, smoking a cigarette, ignores me. Shaken from the confrontation in the store, I can't decide where to go next. In the distance is the rumble of approaching planes. Then the street goes quiet. Everyone around me stops and looks west.

'Where are Poland's planes?' I ask the driver. 'I haven't seen one all morning.' He shrugs.

The droning increases. Panic returns to the street. People hurry off in all directions. Is the shuddering in my chest from the roar of the engines or the racing of my heart? In the doorway of the barber, a young family of four huddles together. The children scream, while their parents desperately try to shield them from the increasing noise.

I tell the driver to take me to the bakery. We arrive as the shadows of the Luftwaffe ripple across the town. The street vibrates with the thunder of aircraft. I step down from the carriage and a sudden paralysis grips me. My knees buckle. I can't breathe. I lean against the wheel to steady myself. What is happening to me? I can't afford to panic. My family can't afford for me to panic. I force myself upright. I can't huddle in a corner. I have to find more food.

For two hours warplanes fly over my head back and forth to Warsaw. Later that afternoon the carriage rocks side to side as it crawls over the cobblestones. The crowds along Skolimow's main street prevent us from moving faster. I watch black smoke billow into the distant sky above Warsaw. The city is burning.

I worry about my younger brother. (Peter stayed behind in our apartment in Mokotow rather than join us in the country.) He doesn't speak Polish. He was forced out of Germany last October when Hitler ordered that all Polish Jews be expelled. I also worry about Sophie's relatives in the city, including her parents and older brother.

It's late and I'm tired. I didn't find any food in the last two shops. I tell the driver to take me back to the cottage. He says, 'That'll cost extra.'

'But I've already paid you two days' rate!'

'It's not enough.'

'Not enough?' I want to beat him senseless. But who am I kidding? I've never been in a fight, don't even know how to fight. What kind of a man am I? Pathetic. We haggle over the amount, and I pay the bastard. He turns the carriage around and takes me out of town.

I take stock of my purchases. In addition to what I bought in the general store, I also acquired two loaves of bread, five dried sausages, half a sack of potatoes and an old cabbage. No milk or eggs. No vegetables or fruit. No beef or fish. Not nearly what I had hoped for, and I've learned nothing about the war.

Sophie and Wanda step out on to the porch, strain etched on their faces. 'You've been gone a long time,' Sophie says.

Wanda walks to the carriage. 'Let me help you carry these inside.'

'Have you heard anything new on the radio? Are the phones working?' I ask.

Sophie shakes her head and then looks with dismay at the food I brought back. I'm embarrassed. 'That's all I could find.'

'I'm sure you did your best.'

We store the food in the kitchen and settle back around the radio. Amidst the static, I find a weak local station. Perhaps they know something now.

'. . . all of Poland, not just Warsaw. Kraków, Poznan, and Lódz all report bombings.' The announcer's voice fades into static. I twist the knob until it clears. '. . . not military targets. They bombed the suburbs of Anin, Wawer and Konstancin. And a small village near Czestochowa is in ruins. Witnesses reported seeing enemy pilots strafe children in the fields near . . .' More static. I turn the knob again. The static eases. The voice returns, '. . . enemy motorized units are advancing quickly east.' Not what I want to hear.

A deep voice interrupts the announcer, 'Sector X, attention! Attention! It approaches.' The station goes silent. No static, just silence.

I look at Sophie and Wanda. 'Did you hear anything like that this afternoon?' They shake their heads.

The voice returns, 'Sector X, attention! Attention! It crossed!' I stare at the radio. What does that mean? The distant rumble of aircraft suggests an answer. The rumble grows steadily louder. But before the planes arrive, the lights and radio die.

2 Sophie Packs

As much as Sophie wants to, needs to, she can't sleep. Anxiety consumes her. Her mind keeps replaying the image of a bomb falling toward the cottage. She sees it clearly: spinning, spiralling, growing larger and larger. It whistles and screams, louder and louder. It crashes through the roof above her, through the bed beside her, through the floorboards beneath her. It explodes, vaporizing everything and everyone. She can't shake off the image.

Climbing out of bed, she stands by the open bedroom window and stares out into the pre-dawn darkness.

What if something happens to the cottage? She hasn't even packed. Three times yesterday planes flew over the cottage, and she didn't think to pack their things. What if they need to flee? Her face flushes with anger. Not being ready is stupid. She'll pack first thing after breakfast. No, the planes might be back before then. She'll do it as soon as everyone wakes. They must be ready to leave in an instant.

The night air cools her cheeks as she looks up at the dark sky. The stars glisten, winking at her from far away. That is where she wants to be, far away from the perils here. It will be light soon. The fading darkness in the east promises as much. The return of the light will surely mean the return of the planes. And the return of the planes will surely mean the return of the noise and the danger, and the panic.

Her hands tremble. Hitler said he wouldn't rest until his armies occupy all of Poland. She can imagine the German Army marching outside her window, can hear the thump-thump-thump of their boots as they trample her garden and destroy her life. And then what? What happens after Hitler's armies occupy all of Poland? What will they do with it? What will they do with her family, her husband, her daughter? O God, what will the German soldiers do with Micki?

She turns toward the bed and whispers to her sleeping husband, 'We should have joined your parents in Palestine. It's my fault we came to Poland, isn't it? My parents live here, not yours. I led you to this place. And now . . .' Her throat tightens and tears well up in her eyes. (*What have I done? I'm the one who didn't want Micki raised in an Ultra-Orthodox home. I didn't want David's mother telling Micki she had to wear a wig to hide her hair. I didn't want David's father telling us the only thing we could do on Shabbat was pray. I didn't want my family subjected to the millions of rules that govern every aspect of Hasidic Jewish lives. Rules born of thousands of years of Jewish history. Old rules for an old time. Rules that have no bearing on our lives today.*)

She feels cold inside. Difficult as life with David's parents might have been, surely it would be better than what they now face, what Micki now faces. They should have emigrated to Palestine despite Sophie's resistance. *If anything happens to Micki, it's my fault.* She covers her face with her hands and weeps.

David rolls over, and she looks up at him. On his back, his face distorted by the shadows of the night, his mouth falls open and he starts to snore, long, loud, relaxed. He's a good man, strong-willed and obstinate at times, but a good man.

She smiles in the darkness, then frowns. Will he be good enough, strong enough, obstinate enough to get them through this? If not, it will be her fault for dragging him to Poland to start a family in the shadow of the Wehrmacht.

She pulls on her dressing-gown. If she is quiet, she can start packing now.

Shortly after dawn, the rumble of enemy planes begin again. Sophie finishes her packing as the windows begin to rattle. The electricity is working now, but the phones remain dead. She spends the day with David and Wanda sitting around the radio while Micki scampers about the house playing with her teddy bear. They hear no news of England or France.

That night, in the quiet following the Luftwaffe's latest flight, the radio reports the German Army's continued advance toward Warsaw. Spies are rumoured to be everywhere. Anyone with a German accent, or caught without a passport, is suspect. Martial law is declared in Warsaw, and an eight o'clock curfew will be strictly enforced. The planes flew overhead today just like yesterday. They attacked at sunrise, then at noon, and again at sunset. Sophie wonders if that will be their pattern.

The electricity dies, and with it the lights and the radio. 'Not again,' Wanda sighs.

David lights a match and touches it to the wick of a candle. 'We might as well go to bed and get some sleep.' Sophie hopes she'll sleep tonight.

During the noon air raid on Sunday, the radio reports that England has declared war on Germany. Sophie thinks it's about time, but keeps the thought to herself.

Six hours later, while they huddle around the dinner table engulfed by the thundering engine noise of the day's last bomb run, the radio announces that France has also declared war on Germany. The announcer calls for all the people of Poland to join together in a unified resistance to the Germans. Sophie shakes her head. 'Another great war.'

David stands up from the table and says, 'I'm returning to Warsaw tomorrow. I need to report to work and find out what's going on.' He looks at Sophie. 'I'm also worried about Peter and your family. I'd like to know how everyone is.' He walks around the table. 'I want you three to stay here. I think it'll be safer, at least for now. Once I decide where is safest for us, I'll come back

11

for you.' He walks out of the living room before anyone can respond.

Sophie doesn't like the idea of being left behind in the country while David goes into the city. She follows him into the bedroom. 'Do you think we should be separated with all that's happening?' She can't remember the last time she questioned one of his decisions.

'I think it's best. At least, I hope it is. It feels right. I have to do something. I can't sit around any longer. We can't hide out here for the entire war, and I have to see what's going on in the city before I can decide what to do.'

She watches him shove things into the bag she packed earlier. He looks scared. That frightens her more. She puts her hands on his back and massages his tense muscles. He turns around, and they embrace. An unusually strong embrace. An embrace of love . . . of need . . . and of fear.

3 Warsaw

I arrive at the railroad station at daybreak. It's packed. There are many men like myself travelling alone with little or no luggage. But I also see entire families, each member carrying an over-stuffed bundle, or a box piled high with possessions. One elderly couple carries a large basket between them that is so full, I'm surprised they can lift it. A peasant woman, wrapped in a tattered shawl, tries to keep her children together while she struggles with a baby carriage in the agitated crowd. Like wild horses in a tight corral, they push and shove against each other. They all want space on the next train to Warsaw.

'The countryside isn't safe,' an old woman says.

'Just south of town,' a young man says, 'parachutists cut the phone lines. They shot 12 children, then escaped into the woods.' Rumours. I'm sick of rumours. I want facts.

A distant rumble signals the beginning of the morning bomb run. The crowd's agitation intensifies. I muscle into the throng. After buying a ticket, I squeeze my way onto the overcrowded train where I stand in the aisle and wait.

As the planes approach, I wonder if the pilots will bomb the train. It would be a logical target. I bend down and look out the window. The people on the platform are trying to push their way onto the train, but there's no more room. Panic shows on their faces. My stomach churns. I'm trapped. If the Germans bomb the train, I can't escape. I drum my fingertips against my leg and pray the bombers will overlook us. An insufferable

13

amount of time elapses before the noise recedes and the train pulls out of the station. My shirt is soaked in sweat.

During the 30-minute ride into the city, I survey the outlying countryside and suburbs. I see no damage to any of the houses or roads, but rural Poland is on the move. Motorcars crammed with people crawl along the crowded road that runs parallel to the tracks. Horses pull wooden carts packed with families and possessions. Peasants ride bicycles with parcels hanging from the handlebars, or walk with rucksacks on their backs and bundles in their arms. They all seek the safety of the city.

As we approach Warsaw, more and more automobiles are abandoned along the side of the road. Petrol is probably no longer available for non-military use, and the owners of the cars have just left them behind when the tanks went dry.

The sky is empty of planes when we pull into Warsaw, but black smoke rises over the eastern section of the city. They must have bombed Praga this morning.

Above the downtown streets, loud speakers hang from lamp-posts and street signs.

'Between air raids,' a male voice blares, 'fight the fires, treat the injured, and dig ditches.' Plastered on every building, large white posters with heavy black lettering call for a general mobil-ization. On each poster, the original date of 8/30 is blotted out. A new date of 8/31 is stamped in purple ink.

Having little cash left, I walk directly to the main post office to withdraw the rest of our savings. A small crowd blocks the entrance. 'They've closed our accounts!' A young man yells at the crowd, shaking his fist. 'They've stolen our money and given it to the army! They're thieves!'

Another man pounds on the doors. 'Open up! You can't take my money!' I stay back. The government of Poland has confis-cated our savings? How are we to live? My hands ball into fists as I fight to control my frustration, prevent it from exploding into rage. Rage won't get my money back. Rage won't feed my family.

14

I walk away. Crime has never been a problem here. We seldom lock our doors. But now, the money I diligently saved to care for my family is gone, stolen by the government – the same government that's supposed to protect us. And there's nothing I can do about it.

I walk towards my place of work. Where could I get some money? Peter, of course. My brother never opened a postal savings account. He keeps all his money hidden somewhere in our apartment in Mokotow. I'll go there.

As I hurry along the sidewalk, people rush by me from every direction. Many have gasmasks hanging from their belts or slung over their shoulders. Like the peasants in the country, the residents of the city are on the move. They carry packages, wear rucksacks, or push carriages piled with belongings. While the people in the country are flocking to the safety of the city, the residents in the city are flocking to the safety of the country. I wish I knew which was better. I take a trolley to Aleja Szucha.

As I enter our fourth-floor apartment, Peter rushes toward me.

'David!' His slender body shakes. Behind his tortoiseshell glasses, his eyes fill with tears. 'Someone stole my money!'

'What?'

He cries. 'Everything I saved was in the pocket of my coat. A year of washing dishes, and it's gone.' My panic returns. I grab his coat off the hook in the vestibule and frantically search through each pocket.

'I've searched it 20 times.'

'Perhaps you put it somewhere else.' Please have put it somewhere else.

'I kept it there in the left pocket. Now what am I going to do?' What's he going to do? What are we going to do?

'I can't believe you kept your money in a coat. What were you thinking?!'

He collapses onto the couch. 'I don't know.'

I collapse beside him. It isn't his fault. 'Don't let it bother you. There's nothing we can do about it now.'

15

'I should have put it in a postal account like you said.'

I shake my head. 'They requisitioned the postal accounts. Our savings are gone, too.'

He looks at me, his face ashen. 'What are we going to do?'

'I don't know.' I stare into the far corner of the room. Despair doesn't help. I look around. 'We'll have to sell whatever we can.'

'What do we have to sell? Who's going to buy it?'

'We have some nice things.' I point across the living room. 'That dining room furniture. Sophie's jewellery. People are always willing to buy nice things, if the price is right.' I walk to the door. 'I have to go to work. Stay here and make a list of everything in the apartment.' I open the door and look back at my brother. 'I'm glad you're safe, Peter. We were worried about you.'

'I disagree,' I tell my co-workers. Three of us are standing in a second-floor storage room. During the noon air raid, we stacked boxes against the outside wall for added protection. The boxes contain a large consignment of knitting wool recently arrived from a supplier in Germany. After the air raid, we stayed behind and smoked cigarettes rather than return to our desks. Without phones, there is no work to do.

Nadaner claps me on the shoulder. 'I'm telling you, anyone with brains will run to Russia. They don't kill Jews like the Germans.' Nadaner is a tall, well-dressed, 46-year-old with thinning hair. He travels throughout Poland selling Bronislaw Poborca's imported textiles. 'That's what I'm going to do. You should, too.'

I shake my head. 'I can't take my daughter on a trip like that. She's still recovering from whooping cough.'

'How do you plan to do it, Nadaner?' Schwalbe is another sales representative, ten years older than Nadaner. 'My family is healthy. Maybe we should go with you.'

Nadaner leans toward Schwalbe, 'I'm going to take the tram east to the end of the line, then walk into the country and buy a horse. If you come, we could buy a wagon.'

'And you'll hope no one robs you along the way,' I tell them. 'I can't believe you'd consider such a dangerous journey.'

'Robbed or not, I won't stop until I'm safely inside Russia,' Nadaner says. 'Being robbed is a small price to pay to avoid death at the hands of the Nazis. Besides, I've heard the German Army is almost here. The city should be evacuated.'

'Rumours,' I scoff. 'You shouldn't listen to them. Who knows the truth?' I consider the possibility that he might be right. Maybe we should go too. But it's not realistic. 'England and France will come to our rescue.' I don't want to hear any more. 'If you'll excuse me, I must go see Panie* Wloch.'

'We all must do what's best for our families. Good luck to you, my friend.'

'Thank you, Nadaner, and good luck to you both.' We embrace briefly.

Mr Wloch, my supervisor in the importing department, is a stooped-over, grey-haired gentleman. 'Here's the salary advance you requested.' He hands me a small stack of currency. 'It's not much, but it's all I could get. I hope it helps.'

'Thank you, Panie Wloch. When this is over, I'll pay you back. I promise.'

'The Nazis won't allow a Jewish-owned business to stay open.' He pats my hand. 'You've been a good employee, David. It's the least we can do for you. Now, go and take care of your family before the evening air raid starts.'

Walking home, I stare up at the smoke billowing into the late afternoon sky. The industrial districts of Warsaw are burning.

I purchase the evening newspaper and am surprised to see that the layout and advertisements haven't changed. On one page, a seductive woman beckons me to smoke her brand of cigarettes. On another, a downtown furniture store offers 20 per

*Mr.

cent off their usually low prices. I study the paper. At last, information other than rumours.

The newspaper describes the devastation of Poland. Photographs of bombed-out villages and burning buildings fill the pages. The dead and wounded include women and children. Refugees are everywhere. I scan for news or pictures of Skolimow, but there is nothing.

Every page contains at least one spy story. One article reports communication lines being cut. Another details false and conflicting orders being issued to several army detachments. Treason is suspected in high quarters. Spies are everywhere. I had better not talk to anyone unless I have to. I tap my coat pocket to ensure my passport is still there.

The paper also recounts many acts of heroism. One story from Westerplatte catches my eye. Three hundred soldiers and two officers are defending their garrison in the Port of Danzig. For three days they have refused to surrender, despite continuous artillery bombardment. Hopelessly surrounded, they continue to fight. Will I have that kind of courage and strength if I need it, if my family needs it? Hopefully I won't have to find out!

The radio greets me when I arrive home. The voice of Panie Starzynski, Warsaw's mayor, proclaims, 'This is not the end of the world; nor is it the end of history.' I walk through the living room, dropping the newspaper on the couch. The familiar surroundings give me comfort. The bombers have yet to release any of their lethal cargo over Mokotow.

'Peter,' I call out over the radio, 'did you put that list together?'

'It's on the table,' he calls back from down the hallway.

'Good, I'll work on finding buyers tomorrow.'

He walks into the living room. 'What can I do?'

'I want you to go to Skolimow. I'm worried about the girls. The newspaper reports widespread bombing and strafing.'

A monotone voice interrupts the radio broadcast, 'Attention. Attention. I announce an air raid alarm for the city of Warsaw. Attention. I announce an air raid alarm for the city of Warsaw.'

18

The dispassionate announcer sounds almost bored. 'Attention. It has passed T point four. Attention.' Before he finishes, sirens begin to wail and anti-aircraft guns bark in the distance.

I glance out of the window. Small puffs of white smoke climb high into the sky. At that moment, for the first time since the invasion started, my anger and anxiety are gone. I feel . . . nothing. Things happening around me no longer carry any threat. It's as if my life is unfolding on a distant cinema screen while I observe it from a comfortable seat in the darkened balcony. As the familiar sound of enemy planes grows louder, I mechanically follow Peter down the stairs to join our neighbours in the basement.

Two hours later, we return to the apartment. Once again, no bombs fell on Mokotow. We share a sandwich for dinner and go to bed. I collapse into a sound sleep.

During the next morning's air raid, I again follow Peter down into the basement. In the kitchen afterwards, we put what is left of our stored food into a small box: a bit of cocoa, some chocolate, a little sugar, a package of condensed milk and a few canned goods. I had thought there was more.

'I haven't slept in days,' Peter confesses. Dark rings encircle his bloodshot eyes. 'Every night, I ask myself the same question. Why am I here? I've no future in Poland, even if the Germans don't come. I can't figure out the language. And I certainly don't want to wash dishes for the rest of my life.'

I squeeze his shoulder. 'Don't ask yourself that question. It'll drive you crazy. Focus on the matters at hand. Survive today. Who knows about the future?' We walk through the living room. I put my arm around him and feel him trembling. 'Be careful.' After he's gone, I clean the kitchen and leave for work.

Surrounded by the chaos in the streets, I wonder if there's any hope of us getting out of Poland. Perhaps the American embassy could help. It isn't far out of my way . . . When I get there, an endless line of people confronts me. The line surrounds

19

the building and stretches down the street. I walk a few blocks towards the end, then stop. How can we emigrate to America? We have no sponsor living in the United States, and we have little money. Even if I did have money and a sponsor, emigration would take time. With the Nazis marching toward us, there is no time. Never again, I promise myself. Never again will I wait so long to act.

When I arrive at work, I find Bronislaw Poborca's doors closed and locked. *Scheisse!* Now what am I going to do?

I slump against the wall and slide down to the pavement. I shouldn't really be surprised. There was no work yesterday. During the brief time the phones were working, the lines were overloaded with emergency traffic. Business calls were impossible to complete. We had no mail to open, no customers to help, no orders to fill. Like our postal savings account, my job is a casualty of war.

I look around. The street is chaotic, with people running in all directions. Should I return to Skolimow, get my family together, pack up and run like these people? But run where? Russia? I can't imagine it. Perhaps we can hide in the country. But we'll still need money for food.

I climb to my feet and walk north. In a daze, I stroll along the sidewalk, hands in my pockets. I watch the commotion in a state of emotional detachment. A group of men my age stand in a ditch. They implore me to help them dig, but I walk past without saying anything. Crossing the street, I pass under the electrical tram wires and decide to ride up to my brother-in-law's house. (I promised Sophie I'd check on her brother's family.) Perhaps Henryk might know of some work I could get paid to do.

When I arrive, I rap the cold brass knocker against the wooden door. Returning my hands to my pockets, I rock back and forth on the balls of my feet and stare up into the smoky sky. The Germans will be making their lunchtime bomb run soon.

The door clicks open, and I turn to see Sophie's sister-in-law standing in the doorway. She smiles at me in surprise. 'David, how wonderful to see you.' Even during an invasion, her tall, slender body is impeccably dressed. Her silky-black hair rests gently on her ample bosom. She swings open the door. 'How are you? Where are Sophie and Micki? Come in, please. Come in.'

Arm in arm, we walk down the hallway towards the living room. Unlike many beautiful women, Stephanie Walfisz exhibits no sign of arrogance or self-admiration. Of all Sophie's relatives, Stephanie is my favourite – a passionate, charitable woman.

'Sophie and Micki are still in Skolimow,' I tell her. 'I returned yesterday. Peter left this morning to be with them.'

As we enter the living room, Sophie's older brother stands and extends his hand. 'David, how are you?' Henryk's long, lean body towers over me.

Halina, their 11-year-old daughter, peeks out from behind Henryk's chair and smiles. 'Hello, Uncle David.'

'Hello, little one.' I shake Henryk's hand. 'I'm fine, but Poborca closed. I thought I'd see how you're doing.'

'Phillips closed, too.' His voice sounds hollow as if he's in shock. All the businesses are closed, except for a few markets that still have food to sell.' He waves his hand toward the sofa. 'Have a seat.'

That evening, Henryk pushes his empty dinner plate towards the centre of the table. 'I'm telling you, I don't like the idea of you leaving my sister and niece in the country.'

'I think they're safer there,' I say.

He sets his linen napkin on the table. 'I disagree. Entire villages have been bombed to dust. How many bombs have fallen in your neighbourhood? None. The same here. Why? Too many better targets. Over 300,000 Jews live in our Jewish communities. Why would the Nazis waste bombs on a Catholic neighbourhood like Mokotow or here in the central part of the city? But if they have bombs left, they have to drop them somewhere. And Skolimow is between here and the border.'

21

'I suppose you're right. Besides, with them out there, I feel cut off and alone.'

Stephanie leans toward me. 'Sophie probably feels the same way.'

Henryk says, 'And if anything happens to her, you won't even know about it.'

'You should go and get them, David,' Stephanie says, frown lines burrowing deep into her brow. 'Sleep here tonight, then go for them in the morning.'

'There's an extra bed in my room, Uncle David,' says Stasiek, their 14-year-old son.

I place my napkin on the table. 'I'll leave first thing tomorrow.'

4 Reunited

Inside the station the next morning, I watch the sunrise through a hole in the building. A corner of the wall lies in a pile of debris. The station is full of refugees and soldiers. I need all my strength to force my way to the ticket counter. An obese stationmaster in a dirty uniform greets me, 'Some of the trains are still running, but I can't say when they'll get here, and I can't say when they'll leave.'

By the time I reach the cottage, the late afternoon sun is baking the countryside. Dirt is streaked on my face in dried rivulets. Peter emerges. 'You're back? Is anything wrong?'

'I think Mokotow is the safest place for us right now,' I tell him. 'But we must hurry. The last train leaves within the hour.'

We get ready quickly. Peter and I each wear over-stuffed rucksacks and carry small boxes. Sophie wears a smaller rucksack. Wanda pushes Micki in the pram. Micki clutches her teddy bear with both arms. We hurry out of the door and just catch the last train to Warsaw.

Once inside the blacked-out city, we take one of the few trams still running south. Two kilometres from our apartment, the conductor tells us to get off. 'We don't service the outlying suburbs anymore,' he says.

In the darkness of Mokotowska Street, I lead us past civilian volunteers digging trenches down the middle of the road. The ditches stretch from the suburbs out towards the countryside. Jackhammers pound ceaselessly on the pavement.

23

'Why are they digging up the streets?' Wanda yells above the din.

'For shelter during air raids,' I yell back. 'And if the Germans attack, they hope they'll stop the tanks.' I doubt they will, but don't say so.

We pick our way around the trenches and rubble. As Peter and I lift the baby carriage over a large chunk of debris, he yells, 'We should get out of here!'

'And go where?' He doesn't answer.

When we arrive home, Sophie collapses on the couch. Wanda takes Micki back to her bedroom while Peter and I use dark paper to black out the windows. 'You finish the windows,' I say to Peter. 'I'll make some coffee. Wanda, would you like some coffee?' I call down the hallway.

'Please.'

'Sophie?' I turn the light on in the kitchen, but hear no response. After starting the coffee, I walk back into the living room and sit by her. 'Are you all right?' She looks at me with vacant eyes, but says nothing.

'Sophie? Are you all right?'

'I don't know,' she whispers. 'Nothing seems real anymore. I feel as if this is all a dream. I'm watching it, but it has nothing to do with me.' I put my arms around her and draw her to my chest.

'Everything is going to be all right. Don't worry. Everything will be fine.'

'Will I ever wake up,' she asks.

The doorbell rings, followed immediately by a loud knock. Peter opens the door, and a high-pitched, angry voice says 'What's going on in here?'

Peter jumps back against the wall, too afraid to move. I turn toward the tall, angry man. He is wearing a blue policeman's uniform. His large black moustache covers most of his mouth. 'Is something wrong?' I ask. He looks at me suspiciously.

'Let me see your identification.' He turns toward Peter. Peter doesn't move. He steps forward, placing his hand on the butt of his revolver. 'Identification. Now! You understand Polish, don't you? Or do you only *sprechen Deutsch*?'

Before I can respond, Wanda enters the room with Micki crying in her arms. 'What's going on?' she asks him. 'You've woken the baby.'

He turns toward her, relaxing slightly. 'Who are you people?'

'I'm Wanda Szcepanska.' She touches Sophie's shoulder. 'This is Sophie Götzel. That is her husband David, and that's his brother Peter. This is their daughter Micki.'

'Where are you from?'

'Warsaw. I've been the Götzels' nanny since I left school two years ago.'

'What about these two?' He points at Peter and me. She explains our family heritage while we hand him our passports. He studies them closely. 'So, you're all Jewish?'

'The Götzels are Jewish. I'm Catholic.'

He hands back our passports. 'I saw light coming from the windows. If I can see light from the street, the Germans can see it from the air.'

'I'm sorry. We've just arrived from Skolimow.' She nods toward the pram, then the windows as she bounces Micki on her hip. 'As you can see, we blacked out the windows.'

'You must do better.' He clicks off the lights. 'No light must escape,' he says, feeling his way out the door.

After eating a quick meal of bread and jam in the dark, we go to bed. Sophie lies on the bed staring at the ceiling as I undress.

'Are you all right,' I ask.

She rolls away from me and speaks to the wall, 'Please don't ask me that anymore.' I'm afraid I'm losing her, but I've no idea what to do about it.

A few hours later, she shakes me awake. 'David! The porter's wife just told us every man in the building must go down to the street immediately. The Germans have reached the defence works! You must erect barricades.'

I climb out of bed. 'Tell Peter to get ready.'

'I did already.'

I pull on my trousers. 'The Germans have reached the defence works already? Didn't the Polish Army slow them down at all?' I can hear shouting from the street below.

Wanda steps into the doorway with Micki asleep on her shoulder. Peter peeks over Wanda's head.

'Everything's going to be fine,' I say with more confidence than I feel. 'Put Micki back in bed. Let's go, Peter.' We rush down the hallway and I finish dressing in the lift.

Outside, dozens of anxious men stand in the dark street. A militia man directs us to a trench on Mokotowska Street. A man at the trench tells us to pile cobblestones onto the barricade at the other end of the street. We go to work. The barricade consists of cobblestones stacked on a large pile of dirt, a couch, a few chairs, a table, and various small appliances. Crossbeams support it all. I can't believe they actually think this garbage might stop the German Army.

As I carry the heavy cobblestones, I ask myself why I didn't apply earlier for emigration, push harder for approval. What can I do now to ensure our safety?

Within an hour, my hands are bleeding, my back aches and my arms and legs cry out for rest. I'm an office worker, not a manual labourer! Peter looks worse. My thoughts turn to how we might get out of hauling any more cobblestones to that worthless pile of junk they call a barricade. I can't think of a way to quit.

Later, I begin to wonder why the militia has us working on Mokotowska Street. If the Germans reached the defence works of Mokotow, what routes might they take into the city? As I think about it, I realize the trench we're digging, and the barricade we're building, will divert the tanks onto Aleja Szucha, directly to our doorstep. We will have to move to a safer location, and we must go tonight. But where? The best place has to be Henryk and Stephanie's. Sophie's brother and sister-in-law are the most likely to take us in when we show up un-announced. And they live in the central part of the city. Warsaw will certainly surrender before the fighting gets that far. But when will we be released from barricade duty?

Another hour passes before the sprawling, two-metre-high mound of stone, dirt, and rubbish blocks the entire road. As a finishing touch, we tip a trolley car onto its side in the centre of it. The ditch stretches out from under the trolley car, down the middle of the street, and out into the darkness. The man in charge looks at our work, wishes everyone good luck, and tells us to go home. I walk quickly away.

'Come on, Peter. We have to hurry.' I explain my plan.

'Are you kidding? I can hardly walk!'

'We have no choice.'

Sophie sits bolt upright on the sofa when I slam the front door and rush inside. 'Sophie, quick! Wanda! We must hurry.' She follows me down the hall.

Wanda steps out of Micki's room. 'What is it?' I explain the situation. Sophie looks incredulous.

It is well after midnight when we set off down the dark streets. Despite the hour, hundreds of people rush about Mokotow. I push Micki in the pram. Peter carries the same box he took to, and brought back from, the cottage. Sophie and Wanda wear rucksacks. Half an hour into our trek, Micki screams, 'Teddy! Where's Teddy?'

I stop. 'Sophie, have you got Micki's teddy bear?'

She turns to Wanda, 'Did you pack Teddy?'

'It's not in the pram? Oh my God. I'm so sorry.' She turns around. 'I'll go and get it.'

I stop her. 'It's too late now. Micki will be fine.'

Micki wails for two hours before falling asleep. We continue marching through the blackened streets. As I walk, I wonder if trekking my family across the city is really necessary. Am I needlessly placing them in danger? I finally push the question out of my mind. At least I'm doing something.

Smoke hangs above the building tops, glowing orange from fires in the northern part of the city. Ash, floating like grey snow on the cool night breeze, settles in our hair and on our eyelashes. My legs and back cry out for rest. But I push on until the eastern sky begins to lighten. After a five-hour journey, we arrive at Henryk's. I knock softly on the door. A moment later, Sophie's mother opens it.

'Sophie?' She wraps her arms around Sophie's neck. 'I was so worried. It's all so terrible, isn't it? They say Kraków fell yesterday. Father went to the sanitorium. He isn't well.' The focus of her eyes darts about as if following the flight of an invisible insect.

'Let's get inside,' I say, squeezing by her. 'We're all very tired.'

'David? Sophie?' Stephanie stands in the hallway wearing a dressing-gown.

'Stephanie, I'm so sorry to impose on you,' I say. 'We heard the Germans were advancing on Mokotow. We had nowhere else to go.'

Smiling weakly, she says, 'You're always welcome here. Help me move the children into the living room. You can have their room.'

'I should go to my apartment,' Wanda says. 'You'll have more room.'

I turn to her, 'Sleep first. Peter and I have to register for the mobilization. We'll take you then.'

We all settle quickly into bed. When the air raid sirens sound, I roll over and ignore them. I'm asleep before the anti-aircraft guns fire their first rounds of the day.

To register for the mobilization, Peter and I stand in a long line of men outside the barracks of the Warsaw garrison. We arrived shortly after the Germans' morning bomb run and now roast in the mid-morning sun.

Early yesterday, Sophie's two elderly aunts arrived at Henryk's, both of them tearful and frightened. Their arrival brought to 12 the number of family members hiding inside the small flat. After we had rearranged the basement to fit in another mattress, the air raids started. They continued constantly throughout the day, keeping everyone inside. Before getting in line this morning, we walked Wanda home. That was two hours ago.

Peter glances down the line then looks at me. Sweat drips off the tip of his nose. 'How much longer do you think?' he asks. I shrug. The line inches forward. When we finally make it inside the barracks and reach the front of the line, a fat bald soldier looks up from his desk. The flab under his chin hides his collar, and the buttons on his uniform strain to hold his shirt closed. 'Names?'

'David and Peter Götzel,' I say.

'Nationality?'

'Polish.'

'Where do you live?'

'Number 30, Aleja Szucha, in Mokotow.'

He eyes Peter. 'Can't he talk?'

'My brother doesn't speak Polish.'

His eyes narrow to puffy slits. 'If you're Polish, as you claim, why is your accent German and your brother doesn't speak our language?' I hand him our passports and start explaining. A young policeman walks over and whispers something to our interrogator. The soldier asks, 'Can anyone here drive a car?'

'I used to drive a taxi in Paris,' I say. (I first met Sophie at the Sorbonne University. It seems like a lifetime ago now.)

He nods. 'The police commissioner at division 16 needs a driver.' He hands me a registration paper. 'Go with this man. He'll take you there. Tell your brother to go home. If he can't speak Polish, we've no use for him.'

I explain things to Peter. He's happy to return to Henryk's. I follow the policeman outside.

At police headquarters half an hour later, I hand a tall dark-haired policeman my registration. He glances at it, and hands it back. 'Have a seat.' He motions to a wooden bench against the wall. The stone wall feels cool against my back. My stomach rumbles. 'Is there anywhere I might get something to eat?' I ask him.

'No, but I have some bread left over from lunch. You want it?'

'Very much.' As I return to the bench, the sirens sound. The policeman at the desk ignores them. I turn my attention to the wedge of white bread in my hand.

After devouring the bread, I read the newspaper – not much more than a newsletter now: one page, no advertising. There are wild stories of Polish military victories; no mention of setbacks. It is all propaganda. Setting the paper aside, I pace back and forth in front of the bench and pray that Sophie and Micki are safe. With each new air raid, my pace quickens.

Late in the day, the policeman hands me an envelope. 'Take this to the fifteenth precinct. Use the blue car.' He hands me a key, identification papers, and a hat. 'Get back here right away. The commissioner should be ready to go home then.'

'Hello, Sophie?' I yell into the phone that night.

'David? Are you all right?' she asks.

'Fine. I've been trying to get through for hours.'

'I was worried when you didn't come back with Peter. It's so late now.'

'I'm running errands for the police commissioner.'

'What's that got to do with defending Warsaw?'

'I don't know, but it's better than building barricades.'

'Where are you?'

'At home. The commissioner's apartment isn't far from here. How is everyone?'

'It's too crowded. We want to come home.'

'I think you're safer there, but have Peter come back here. That will give you more room.'

'I don't want to stay here. My aunts are driving me crazy.'

'Just a while longer. You'll be fine.'

'I'm not so sure.'

'We shouldn't tie up the line. I'll call again tomorrow. I love you, Sophie.'

'I love you, too, David.'

After I hang up, an artillery shell whistles over the apartment and explodes in the distance. The Germans must be close enough to lay siege to the city. So much for any calm between air raids.

Two weeks later, Peter and I sit in the kitchen. I stare at the candle on the table. Its flame dances above the tiny pool of wax. 'They bombed the northern section of the city today,' I tell him. 'The worse yet.'

'That section's all Jewish, isn't it?' I nod.

He shakes his head. 'On Yom Kippur. That's no accident.'

'They dropped leaflets, too. "We'll give you a Day of Atonement you'll never forget."'

'The radio said they destroyed the power station,' he says.

'I doubt we'll have phones or electricity until it's over.' I stand and pace across the kitchen. 'I'm worried about Sophie and Micki. Henryk's home is too close to the destruction. And if the Germans were going to invade the city, they'd have done it by now. I think Sophie and Micki would be safer here.'

'Why don't you drive over there and bring them home?'

'If I use the car for personal reasons, they'll shoot me. Will you go and fetch them?'

'I'll leave in the morning and bring them back on Monday.'

5 Return to Mokotow

Early on Monday morning, Sophie stands in Henryk's basement. Mahogany furniture lines the walls, but fails to block out the sounds of war. Sirens blare. Anti-aircraft guns chatter. Engines roar.

Peter stands by the door, shifting his weight back and forth. Stephanie sits next to the door on a mattress, her back resting against a bureau. Stasiek and Halina are asleep beside her. In a chair next to the mattress, Sophie's mother knits. Across the room, the Nowinski aunts sit with their heads together, complaining about one thing or another. Wanda, who returned three days ago after a bomb destroyed her apartment, sits in a chair against the other wall. Her suitcase rests beside her. Micki sits on her lap.

Henryk stands next to Sophie. There are deep lines around his tired eyes and furrows across his brow. Three weeks of war have etched years into his face.

'I don't think you should go,' he says. 'Stay here with us.'

Sophie shakes her head. 'It's too crowded. And David thinks we'll be safer at home.'

'At least wait until this raid is over.'

'When the planes leave, the shelling will start.'

He gently strokes her arm. His voice is soft and soothing, 'Remember when you first arrived? You and David struggled so hard to learn Polish, and he was worried sick about finding a job. So many complaints.'

She hugs her brother. 'We wouldn't have made it without you and Stephanie.'

'Having you live with us was a happy time for me.'

She lays her head on his chest, his wool shirt warm against her cheek. 'And we thought we were an imposition.'

He laughs. 'You're always welcome in my house, *Kleiner Fisch.*'* He looks across the room. 'Poor Micki. Her uncle hasn't had much time to play with her.'

Sophie pats him on the arm. 'There will be other times. We must be going.' Wanda hands Micki to Sophie, and they all walk upstairs. In the living room, Sophie puts Micki in the pram and rubs her stomach until she giggles.

'Here we go, little one,' Peter says and places a box across the carriage to protect her. She starts crying. He removes the box. 'I don't think this will work.'

'And I don't think you should go,' Henryk says.

Sophie scoops Micki into her arms. 'Sorry, Henryk.' She kisses him on the cheek and walks outside. 'We'll see you when it's over!' She yells above the whine of air raid sirens and the distant explosions of anti-aircraft fire, 'Take care, big brother!' Peter follows, pushing the pram, the box now back on top. Wanda walks beside Peter, carrying her suitcase.

The sun has not yet climbed above the building tops. The smell of smoke fills the shadows. To the north, German warplanes weave their way between white puffs of anti-aircraft fire, but directly overhead the brilliant blue sky is clear. Sophie marches south, thinking that with luck, they should be home by noon.

Something whistles over her head, and an explosion rocks a building half a block away. The shock wave thunders in her ears. Flames lick out of the windows. Smoke billows into the sky. Micki starts crying, and Sophie wonders if she's doing the right thing. But who knows what is right? If David thinks Mokotow is safer, then she'll trust his judgement. She hugs

---

*Little fish.

Micki and says, 'It's OK, little one. Everything's going to be fine.'

Peter hurries beside her with the pram. 'Maybe we should go back!'

'We're going home!' She hurries forward, comforting Micki as she goes.

An hour later, a hundred planes fly out of the north toward the four of them. Anti-aircraft fire begins exploding directly over their heads.

'Take cover!' Peter yells. Abandoning the pram in the middle of Marshalkowska Street, he races into the entrance of an office building. Sophie leans forward to shield Micki as metal shards rain onto the cobblestones around her. Something strikes her on the shoulder, and her arm goes numb. She shifts Micki to her other arm. She isn't sure which way to run and is too afraid to look up.

Wanda appears beside her, holding the suitcase above their heads. 'Come on!' She yells. Sophie follows her to the doorway where Peter has taken cover. 'We'll never make it!' he cries.

An explosion causes part of the building across the street to collapse. Sophie turns to shield Micki from the blast and feels a monstrous, scorching heat on her back. Micki wails. Another bomb explodes down the block, then another. Shock waves pummel them. Sophie looks up and sees flames leaping high into the air. The next moment is calm, and she quickly checks Micki for injuries. Finding none, she hands her to Wanda, and then feels under her sweater where the metal hit her shoulder. The skin isn't broken. She flexes her hand and senses the feeling returning to her arm.

They huddle in the doorway for two hours while the planes fly overhead and bombs fall all about the commercial district. Flak impacts the street like jagged hailstones, riddling the box that still sits atop the pram. Smoke drifts between the buildings like a black fog.

When the sky clears, they set off again. Along both sides of the street buildings are burning. They cover their mouths with handkerchiefs and press on through the smoke. Suddenly, artillery rounds begin whistling above their heads, followed by explosion after explosion.

'They're aiming at the businesses,' Sophie yells. 'Let's get off Marshalkowska.'

'We can cut over to Ujazdowska,' Wanda yells. 'Maybe the park is safer.'

Sophie nods. 'Let's try it!'

From Ujazdowska Street, they duck into the park and turn south. Wanda was right. This area is quiet, and they move quickly through the pine trees. As the sun sinks towards the smoke-filled horizon, they run through Lubelski Square, Sophie far in the lead, Micki asleep in her arms.

'Almost home,' Sophie whispers. Rounding the aviator statue in the centre of the square, she stumbles on something in the shadow at the statue's base. Thinking she kicked someone, she stops. 'I'm sorry. I didn't see you.' Stepping forward, she looks closer.

Lifeless eyes stare out of the darkness from a woman's body. Her right arm and part of her torso are gone. One of her lungs is spilled on the ground. It lies in a dark pool at Sophie's feet. Sophie jumps back, stomping her feet to get the blood off her shoes. Something lies in the crook of the dead woman's elbow. It's the top half of an infant.

Sophie's legs go limp. She pitches to the side and braces herself against the statue. She can't breathe. Trying to inhale, she gasps uncontrollably, then vomits. Twice.

'Oh my God!' Wanda cries as she rounds the statue.

'Don't look,' Peter says. 'Keep moving. We're almost home.'

Peter and Wanda grab Sophie's arms to support her, carry her forward. Her legs are still numb, but she gets them moving. She looks up and sees Mokotowska Street in flames.

Inside our darkened apartment, I pace from one end to the other. Lights from neighbourhood fires flicker on the walls and ceiling. Noise and smoke filter through the broken windows and hang in the air, tormenting me. Why did the Germans pick today to bomb the southern suburbs? I've heard nothing from Peter. Did he make it to Henryk's? From behind the wheel of my car yesterday, I watched the Nazis disembowel the centre of the city. If Peter had made it, he would have been convinced Mokotow was safer. But if they tried to return today . . .

I don't want to think about that. I can only hope they're all right, but I've no way of knowing. The phones are dead. The radio broadcasts are all propaganda. The newspaper stopped publishing. I've no electricity, little water and less food. The only available information is whatever sound the wind carries. During a brief calm between explosions, I stand by the window and listen. Gunfire cracks in the distance. I return to pacing.

Suddenly the door opens, and Sophie staggers in with Micki asleep in her arms. Soot, dirt and ash cover them both. Her clothes are torn, her shoes filthy. 'Sophie! Micki!' I bury my face in her neck and taste the salty ash on my lips.

Peter and Wanda trail in looking as bedraggled as Sophie. 'Thank you, Peter,' I say, clapping him on the shoulder. Ash billows from the impact. I look into their dirty faces and my throat tightens. 'I was so worried,' I whisper, swallowing my tears. I brush Sophie's hair back away from her face. 'Are you all right?'

'Mokotow is on fire,' she says softly. 'Houses are burning. People dying.'

Light flickers in the dark hollows of her eyes. She doesn't want to answer any more questions. There's no time anyway. We're still in danger.

'We should go to the basement,' I say.

She shakes her head. 'We were already down there. It's not safe. Only one exit and too many people. I don't want Micki trapped down there if the building starts burning.'

A blinding orange flash illuminates the room, followed immediately by an explosion that shatters the remaining glass in the windows. Micki wakes with a howl. The building next door collapses with a tremendous crash. Sophie holds Micki against her chest and turns her back to the noise. I feel the heat on my face as flames rage into the sky.

'Let's go across the hall,' Wanda yells. 'The neighbours are in the basement.'

'Quickly!' I call, motioning everyone out.

We scamper into the hallway of our neighbour's flat and lie on their hardwood floor. Sophie wraps herself around Micki who screams in objection. I wrap myself around Sophie. Peter and Wanda squeeze along the baseboards on each side and wrap their arms around the three of us. Artillery shells explode. The floorboards shudder. The acrid smell of smoke grows stronger.

In anguish, I whisper, 'Hear, O Israel: the Lord is our God, the Lord is One! I've done what I can to protect my family. Now, I ask for Your help. If You'll get us through this war, I promise to live the rest of my life by Your commandments.' At the sound of another explosion, my body shivers. 'Into Your hands I commend my spirit.'

An eternity passes before the noise subsides and Micki stops screaming. I've lost all feeling in my shoulder from lying on the floor.

Sophie whispers to me, 'Tomorrow is Micki's birthday.'

I am more worried about living through the night than anything happening tomorrow. I think for a moment about the date. 'Yes, it is.'

'What can we give Micki for her birthday?'

'Now is not the time to worry about such things,' I say, stroking her hair.

'We must give Micki a present for her birthday.'

'Relax, *Häschen*, maybe you should try and sleep.'

'I know.' She sits up and hands Micki to me. 'I'll be right back.'

'Sophie, no!' I reach for her, but she slips from my grasp. 'Sophie!' She scurries toward the door on all fours.

'Where's Sophie going?' Wanda asks, her face now next to mine. 'I don't know,' I say, fearing my wife has lost her mind. Another explosion rocks the building.

Sophie crawls across the hall and into her apartment. Heat and smoke fill the living room, stinging her eyes, burning her throat. If she can find Micki's teddy bear, it would make a perfect birthday present. Glass splinters bite into her hands and knees as she crawls down the hallway. She doesn't care. At any moment, they could all be killed. She stands and walks defiantly to the back of the apartment. She'll make her daughter happy, at least one more time.

Teddy isn't on Micki's bed or in her closet, but it has to be here somewhere. She rips the drawers out of the bureau, then tips it over in frustration. Where is Teddy? An explosion knocks her off her feet. A stabbing pain shoots through her elbow as she hits the floor. Lying on her side, she kicks the corner of the bed.

'Where are you, Teddy?' She screams, then starts to cry. She can't do something as simple as find her daughter's toy bear. Pulling her knees to her chest, she stares across the floor through her tears. In the shadow under the bed, two specks of light twinkle. 'Teddy?' She scoots forward and reaches toward the twin reflections. Her fingers close around woolly fur, and she takes Micki's bear from the darkness. She laughs and jumps to her feet. Clutching the bear to her chest, she runs back across the hall. David gives her a stern look as she lies down beside him. Micki's back is to her. Sophie places the toy in Micki's arms. 'Happy birthday, little one.'

'Teddy,' Micki squeals, hugging the stuffed animal. 'O, Teddy, I missed you!'

The floorboards reverberate with another explosion.

At daybreak, I step into the quiet street and look around. The building next to ours, and one across the street, are smouldering ruins. And yet, the five-storey structure that houses my family

– the tallest building in the neighbourhood, is undamaged. I bow my head, squeeze my hands to my chest, and whisper, 'Thank You.' Air raid sirens wail, so I hurry down the street to my car.

That afternoon, I drive up Elektoralna Street to Henryk's. Since my last errand brought me into his neighbourhood, I feel justified with a brief visit. For the moment, the Germans are shelling the other side of the Vistula River.

Sophie's aunts answer my knock. 'Oh David, what are we going to do without Henryk?' One cries. The other dabs her eyes with a crumpled handkerchief.

'What do you mean?' I ask.

'Henryk, poor Henryk. What are we going to do without him?' They bawl.

'What are you talking about?' But they only cry louder.

In the living room, Sophie's mother weeps hysterically. Stasiek sits on the couch, his arm around his younger sister. Dirt stains his hands and the knees of his trousers.

I sit across from them. 'What happened?'

'I came upstairs this morning to get Grandma some water,' Halina says softly. 'I was only trying to help. Father was standing there,' she points to the doorway, 'something exploded in the backyard . . .' Tears fill her eyes.

'A piece of glass struck his throat,' Stasiek says, nodding his head toward a broken window. His eyes drift down to the floor where a large stain darkens the wood. 'We couldn't stop the bleeding.' He looks up at me. 'I buried him in the garden.'

At two o'clock the next afternoon the shelling stops. I park my car and look around. The smoky grey sky is clear of planes. The city is quiet for the first time in two weeks. Is it possible? Could our nightmare be over? I turn on the radio. A monotone voice announces a 24-hour armistice to permit peace negotiations and burial of the dead.

I rest my head against the steering wheel.

6 Occupation

Four days later, on Sunday morning, 1 October 1939, the Germans march into Warsaw. A cold front moved through the region yesterday bringing an icy wind that now disperses the acrid smell of smouldering destruction. The city's residents, wrapped in winter coats, line the main boulevard. We stand behind the crowd. No one cheers.

Row after row of shiny helmets, polished jackboots and fixed bayonets glisten in the cold sun, as battalion after battalion marches past. Fourteen impeccably clean grey-green uniforms are perfectly aligned in each row. The thump-thump-thump of their heels echoes off the buildings. Left-right, left-right, left-right. They parade in sterile synchronization.

'Come on,' I say. 'We don't have to watch this. We can take the long way to Stephanie's.' Peter and Wanda follow us, Wanda pushing Micki in the tattered pram.

That afternoon, Sophie kneels in the garden and places three pink carnations on a long mound of fresh earth. The small brass plate lying on top reads: *Henryk Walfisz*. The plate was on his front doorway. It was the only headstone we could find.

'How are you going to play with Micki now, Henryk,' she whispers, her finger caressing the letters on the brass plate. 'You know, it's almost as if all I need do is knock, and I could be with you again . . .' She covers her face and cries. I kneel beside her and place my arm around her shoulders.

Sophie's mother sinks to her knees and stretches her arms across the grave. 'Henio, my child! My son, Henio!'

I help Sophie to her feet and we walk back to the house.

Dressed in full mourning, Henryk's family watches from the doorway. Stephanie's dark, puffy eyes stare into the distance while tears stream down her pale cheeks. Halina, her arms wrapped around her mother, leans against Stephanie's side. Stasiek stands behind them, one hand on Halina's shoulder, the other on Stephanie's. Sophie and I wrap our arms around the three of them. We all weep.

A few days later, I watch Sophie look at the empty space where her polished-oak dining room set had been. The furniture was a wedding gift from her aunts. In her gloved hands she holds a single loaf of bread – her reward for two hours of queuing.

'I see the neighbours finally agreed to buy,' she says.

We all wear coats and gloves. Warsaw is still without electricity, gas, or running water. Clouds form in the still air of the apartment as we breathe. Despite repeated attempts to seal our broken windows, the arctic chill seeps in.

I put my arm around her. 'I'm sorry about your dowry. I know what it meant to you.'

She leans against me. 'After what we've been through, it's not important.'

'Peter and I are going out for food.'

'Be careful. I saw soldiers forcing people to clean up the streets.'

'Don't worry, *Häschen*. We'll be fine.' I kiss her on the cheek, and we leave.

Three hours later, we have acquired only two tins of sardines, three cucumbers, an onion and some horsemeat. The shops we found open were mostly empty.

On our way home we pass a dozen men standing on the sidewalk reading announcements posted on the wall of a building. I look over the official notices. The first one says the Germans have come to bring peace and order to our stricken city. What a slap in the face. The next one says everyone is to return to work immediately. All the Poles, Ukrainians, White Russians and Jews living inside Warsaw will retain their national freedom. Everyone will be treated equally. Another notice announces new property restrictions. To carry firearms, or weapons of any kind, is strictly *verboten* and will be treated as a capital offence. In addition, Jews are no longer allowed to have more than 2,000 zloty in their possession at any time. So much for equal treatment.

'Two thousand zloty isn't much money,' Peter whispers to me.

'Let's go,' I say. I'm carrying more than 2,000 zloty and want to get home to hide it. As we turn to leave, an army truck screeches to a halt beside us.

'*Komm mal hier!*' a German soldier calls to the group, '*Komm! Schnell!*'*

The men gather around the truck as the soldier climbs out from behind the wheel. He says (in German), 'You must clean this street immediately. And that trench over there must be filled before anyone can leave.' The Poles stare at him, confused and afraid.

I interpret, 'He said we have to clean up the street and fill in that trench.'

The soldier smiles and walks up to me. He fingers the rifle slung over his shoulder. The sun reflects off a gold ring on his finger. 'You speak German?' I nod, gripping the sack of food in my arms. I suddenly feel very cold.

'Where are you from?' He asks, leaning his head to the side.

'Baden-Baden.'

'And you moved here to Warsaw?'

'*Ja.*'

'Then you are either a fool, or a stinking Jew. Now get to work!' He kicks me in the thigh, and I stagger sideways. Intense

---

*Come here at once. Come! Hurry up!

pain shoots down my leg. Another kick, this one in the small of my back, knocks me to the sidewalk. My food spills into the street. He turns to the other soldiers climbing out of the truck. 'Look at this clumsy fool!' They laugh.

As the Polish men hurry to work, their feet scatter my food. I scramble to pick it up, my leg and back throbbing. 'He said get to work,' another soldier says, kicking me: a glancing blow to my buttocks. I maintain my footing, but drop my food. I limp over to join the other men, already busy carrying stones and bricks to the trench.

An hour later, I am covered in dirt and sweat. My hands are bleeding. My body aches. Peter is the same. Debris still covers most of the street and sidewalks, and the trench is only a quarter full. As Peter helps me move a chunk of concrete, he whispers, 'Are you all right?'

'I'm not going to make it,' I tell him. 'I have to get away from here.'

'With them watching? How?'

I had been thinking about it for a while. I glance across the street where the corner of a building is collapsed. 'After we drop this in the trench, walk with me to that pile of concrete over there. When the soldiers look away, we run down the alley.'

'They'll shoot us if we run.'

'They'll work us to death if we stay.' We drop the concrete in the ditch and walk across the street. My stomach is in knots. My knees are wobbling. We walk around a large chunk of the wall and act as if we're about to pick it up. The soldiers are talking among themselves, laughing, smoking cigarettes.

'Now,' I whisper. Still hunched over, we back slowly around the building. Once we're out of the Germans' sight, we dash down the alley. As we round the far corner, a soldier on the next street sees us.

'*Halt!*' he shouts. We stop and look at each other. In that frozen moment of time, I reach out to my brother. I want to hold him, protect him.

43

'*Komm mal hier!*' the soldier yells.

Peter and I turn away from each other and sprint in opposite directions. My thigh and back scream in agony from being kicked, but I keep moving. At each corner, I stop and peer around, before dashing down the street. After four blocks, I slow, wipe my face with my handkerchief, and limp the rest of the way home. I don't see Peter.

Sophie looks up from the couch when I enter our apartment. She watches me close and lock the door. My clothes are filthy, my hands caked with blood.

'Where's Peter,' she asks.

A week passes without word from Peter. Then, late one morning, I hear a faint knock on the apartment door. Walking into the foyer, I call out in Polish, 'Who's there?'

'It's me,' Peter's familiar voice replies.

I fling the door open. 'What happened to you? We've been so worried.'

'Peter!' Sophie hurries down the hall. 'Peter's back,' she calls to Wanda in the kitchen, then embraces him. 'Where have you been?'

'After running from the soldiers I met Eva.' He steps aside, revealing a small, stern-looking young woman with thick glasses. They are both wearing rucksacks. 'I've been hiding in her mother's apartment since last week. I was too afraid to go outside.'

'David hasn't gone out either,' Sophie says, motioning for them to enter. 'Wanda and I always take Micki. So far, we've been left alone.'

'It's not safe for men to be on the streets,' I say, then poke my head into the hallway and look around. I close and lock the door.

'It's especially dangerous for Jewish men,' Eva says.

'Come join us for lunch, Eva,' Sophie says.

'Thank you, but I don't have time. I'm leaving immediately for Russia.'

'Are you mad?' I say. 'If you wanted to flee to Russia, you should have done so months ago. You'll be killed for sure if you try it now.'

Eva looks at me, determination on her face. 'I'll never stay here under the Nazis!'

Peter looks at her with admiration. 'I'm going with her. We only stopped to let you know what happened. We can't stay. We have to be out of the city before curfew.'

I see strength in my brother's eyes for the first time in his life. 'Wait a moment.' I run into the kitchen and return, handing him a small parcel. 'Take this loaf of bread with you.'

'I can't take this, David. It's probably the only bread you have. Give it to Micki.'

'It's all we have right now, but I'll go out this afternoon and get more. Take it.' I push the parcel into his hands. '*Shalom aleichem*, Peter.'

'*Aleichem shalom*, David.' We embrace.

It is early November, and I am walking up Marshalkowska Street along the business district. The sun is dropping quickly toward the horizon. I keep my head straight, but my eyes scan constantly for danger ahead while my ears strain for any sound from behind. Next to me a horse struggles to pull a truck up the street – a substitute for the tram that no longer runs. Red Nazi flags now drape from every building. They billow in the late afternoon breeze. Their black swastikas, encircled in white, proclaim German superiority. Copies of official notices are plastered to every wall, the latest announcing that Jews can no longer use what remains of the public transport system.

My costume jewellery sales were unusually good today, and inside the secret compartments of my belt I am once again carrying more money than the law allows. An elderly man rounds the corner of the building and bumps into me. 'Turn around,' he whispers and continues on his way. I immediately reverse my direction and walk the other way. From around the corner behind me, where I would have been walking, I hear a truck brake to a halt. A voice calls, *'Komm mal hier!'* Heavy boots land on the pavement. Distant footsteps break into a run. *'Halt!'* The voice commands. There is a gunshot.

I shove my hands into my pockets and walk faster. I don't look back. A Hasidic Jew steps out from a building and walks toward me. 'Turn around,' I whisper as we pass. He spins on his heels without hesitation and hurries away.

Once home, I hide half the money in the hallway cupboard under Micki's old clothes. Up until now, we've been forced to spend every zloty I earn on food. If I can sell as much jewellery every day as I did today we might even be able to save a little.

'Did you make any money today?' Sophie asks, entering the room.

'Enough to feed us for awhile. How have you been?'

She shrugs. 'Two hours waiting for bread. Another for vegetables. Chopped some wood. Fetched some water.'

'And Micki?'

'Fine. Sleeping. Wanda just put her down.'

'Good, good.' We have this exact conversation every night.

'I heard a report today,' she says, 'The Jews in Łódz can't use the pavement anymore, and they're all required to wear a yellow star on their chest.'

'You must stop listening to rumours. They'll make you crazy. Why on earth would the Germans make Jews do such things? Me, I'd rather drink poison than walk around this city with a sign around my neck telling everyone I'm a Jew.' I go into the kitchen.

She follows me. 'Mother asked if she could stay with us for a while.'

'Move in here?' That's all I need, another mouth to feed.

'She can't stay at Stephanie's anymore. Henryk's memory is too painful for her.'

If Sophie's mother joins us, I'll have to find some way to make more money. But how can I refuse? 'Have her bring her things next week,' I say. Sophie kisses me on the cheek, walks to the sink, and starts washing dishes.

'I saw people walking in and out of Bronislaw Poborca today,' I say. 'They may be back in business. I'll go there tomorrow and see if I can get my old job back.'

The next day I wait in the outer office that used to belong to my former employer. A tall attractive blonde emerges. She looks to be around 40 and wears a tan two-piece suit. 'My name's Janina Joblanska,' she says in Polish as she approaches me, 'I'm the German Kommisar. You wished to speak to me?'

To impress her, I reply, *'Ich möchte gerne wieder hier arbeiten.'**

'I don't speak German.'

I switch to Polish. 'I'm sorry. I used to work here as a clerk, and I was wondering if I might work here again.'

'You speak fluent German?'

I nod. 'French and English as well.'

'And you used to work here?'

'Yes.'

'So, you're Jewish,' she says, frowning. I nod.

'I'm sorry. I'm not allowed to hire Jews.' I feel my body deflate. My shoulders slouch. 'Thank you for your time.'

As I turn to leave, she says, 'But I do need a clerk who can translate, and no one here speaks German. Please have a seat while I talk to my boss.'

Twenty minutes later, I sit in front of the trustee's desk while he strokes his moustache and stares at the ceiling. Miss Joblanska stands to one side. 'Next month,' he says, breaking the silence, 'all Jews in Warsaw will be required to wear identifying armbands.'

'I haven't seen any notices,' Miss Joblanska says.

'You will, and it would cause us problems if Mr Götzel wore one in the office.'

---

*I would very much like to work here again.

'What if I didn't wear an armband while I was here?' I suggested.

'Then you'd be violating the law.'

'But I wouldn't be causing you any problems, would I?'

He looks at Miss Joblanska. She nods. He looks at me. 'He doesn't look Jewish.' He says to Miss Joblanska. 'See to the necessary papers.' He turns back to me. 'We never spoke.'

When I arrive home, I call out, 'Sophie, great news!' I hear the sound of crying from the back of the apartment and hurry down the hall. Sophie is lying on the bed with her face buried in a pillow. Wanda stands beside her.

'What's wrong?' I ask.

Sophie raises her head toward me. Her eyes are red and puffy. 'My father died last night in the sanitorium.' Her eyes fill with tears. I sit on the bed and wrap my arms around her.

'First Henryk, and now Father.' She buries her face in my chest. 'And a new order forbids Jews from changing residence. Mother can't move in with us.'

I stroke her hair. 'I'm sorry about your father, *Häschen*. By spring, though, the war should be over. Your mother can move in with us then. We'll just have to wait until spring.'

7 The Jewish Star

I walk along the right side of the road, snow crunching under my feet. The morning air stings my nose. Above the right elbow of my coat is a white armband. On the armband is a blue, six-pointed star. If I stay on the right side of the road, fewer people can see it.

Under the protection and encouragement of the Nazis, Polish anti-Semitism flourishes. Most Poles now blame the Jews for all the country's problems and consider us sub-human. Since the Germans announced residential searches for weapons, Poles flock to the Gestapo to report their wealthier Jewish neighbours. After ransacking Jewish homes, the Gestapo rewards the Poles with a share of the plunder. Bands of Polish hooligans now roam the city, beating and robbing the easily identified Jewish residents. I mourn the loss of my anonymity . . . and my freedom.

Half a block from Bronislaw Poborca, I duck into a doorway and pretend to tie my shoe. When no one is looking, I slide my armband off my sleeve and tuck it inside my pocket. A moment later, I emerge from the doorway and continue on my way to work.

Later that morning, I sit at my desk in the hallway translating an import letter.

Behind me, Janina Joblanska steps out of her office. 'Have you ever been to the General Trustee's office?' She wears a long grey woollen skirt and matching sweater. Her flaxen hair is pulled back into a single braid.

'Which General Trustee?' There are quite a few.

'The General Trustee for Jewish Property. He's in charge of all the Kommisars running businesses formerly owned by Jews.' I note a hint of disgust in her tone. She is an enigma to me: she hates injustice, tries to be fair, but works for the Nazis. Under other circumstances I think we could have been good friends.

'Is it in the old Chamber of Commerce building?'

She nods. 'Could you take this report to Herr Eisner? He's expecting it by noon, and I've no one else who can deliver it for me.' I agree. As I leave the building, I hug the right side of the street, round the corner, and duck into another doorway. I emerge a moment later with my armband back in place.

'*Halt!*' A voice commands from behind me. Damn! I didn't see the two German soldiers down the street.

'*Komm mal hier, Jude.*'* They are herding Jews onto a truck. I walk up to the soldier who called me and hold out my green labour card. My hands are sweating inside my gloves. If he questions the propriety of a Jew working in a formerly Jewish-owned business . . .

'Such a well-dressed Jew, and with a labour card.' He studies the signature of the Kommisar below the swastika. 'Where do you think you're going, *Jude*?'

'I'm delivering this report to the Chief German Trustee of Jewish Property as directed by my Kommisar.' I hand him Janina's envelope. Not wanting to allow him enough time to think, I state, 'Herr Eisner is expecting this report immediately!'

The sound of my unaccented German rattles him. He looks confused, disappointed. He returns my envelope and labour card and waves me off. 'Very well. Move along.' As I back away, he turns and kicks an old man climbing onto the truck, '*Schnell!*'

Less than an hour later, with my armband safely back inside my pocket, I hurry across the bustling downtown plaza.

---

*Come here at once, Jew.

Warsaw's tallest buildings surround me, and I notice how little they are damaged. It's almost as if the German artillery and bombers had intentionally saved the downtown district for the Nazis.

I enter the old Chamber of Commerce building. After a brief wait in an entrance area on the fourth floor, the receptionist leads me down a wide, brightly lit hallway to a door marked: 'General Trustee for Jewish Property in Occupied Warsaw/Notary.'

A young, attractive secretary with shoulder-length black hair looks up from her desk as I enter. 'May I help you,' she asks me in German.

I step forward and place the envelope on her desk. 'My name is David Götzel. This report is for Herr Eisner.'

'One moment please.' She stands, then jumps back. 'God damn it!' Bending down, she lifts her skirt above her knee, exposing long, smooth legs. She is tall, slender, and shapely. 'I just ruined my stocking. Do you know how difficult these are to come by?'

My mind races, imagining how valuable it could be to have an ally inside the Trustee's office. The city's black market has been growing for months. With enough money, anything is available. 'I understand silk stockings are almost impossible to obtain, but if I'm ever in a position to acquire them, I'd be happy to buy some for you.'

She looks up suspiciously and drops the hem of her skirt. 'A close friend of mine is a high-ranking officer in the Gestapo. He would not look fondly on your advances.'

I step back. 'I . . . I meant no disrespect. It's just . . .' I hesitate. What have I done now? I stare at the floor. My face feels hot. 'It's just that during these difficult times, I believe we can all survive better by helping each other. That's all.'

She studies me for what feels like an eternity. 'OK, Herr Götzel. If you could acquire some stockings for me, I'd be grateful. My name is Fräulein Demske. If you'll wait here, I'll give Herr Eisner your report.' She disappears into the inner office.

I let out a long sigh. I need to be more careful. On the wall is a portrait of Hitler. I sneer and turn my back to it. On the opposite wall is a picture of Hans Frank, the head of Poland's new government. He is responsible for the laws restricting Jewish activities, requiring Jews to wear armbands and the confiscation of Jewish businesses and property. I turn away from his picture as well and look out the window. It's amazing how few buildings are damaged down here.

When I arrive home that evening Sophie hands me a postcard, 'This was delivered through the Red Cross today.' She is solemn and withdrawn. I'm worried about her. She has stopped telling me to be careful, hardly talking at all. I don't know how to help her, and I feel lost because of it. I glance at the postcard. 'Sophie, have you looked at this? My father has sent us immigration visa numbers for Palestine. Our application has been accepted. He says he looks forward to us joining him and Mother soon.'

She looks at me without interest. 'What chance is there of that happening?'

'None now, but perhaps later, after things settle down. Perhaps in the spring.'

She walks into the kitchen without responding. I take the postcard to the hallway cupboard and hide it with our other valuables.

The weather is unusually warm during the spring of 1940. Sweat stings my eyes as I carry the last box down the hot, humid hallway. Janina gave me permission to store some of our possessions in one of the company's back rooms. In February the Nazis ordered the establishment of a Jewish district in the city of Lódz, and rumours of a planned Warsaw ghetto abound. This building is inside what I guess to be the future Jewish district. When I heard the Germans invaded Denmark and Norway in April, I decided to store what I could so it will be available to us in case we're forced to move from Mokotow.

Sophie stands in the tiny storage room surveying the meagre belongings I've piled in the corner. Stacked against the walls, dusty boxes of knitting wool surround her. She looks up as I enter. 'We haven't much left, have we,' she says.

'We have enough.' I wipe the sweat from my forehead with a handkerchief. 'Not as much as some, but more than others. We're still alive. We're still together. That's all that's important.' I wrap my arms around her. She rests her head on my shoulder.

'I don't see how we're going to make it, David.'

'Everything's going to be all right, Sophie. Don't you worry.' I gently stroke her hair. 'By next spring, this should all be over.'

'You said it would all be over by this spring.'

'Next spring for sure.'

On our way home, we stop by the apartment of Mr Wloch, my former supervisor. The three of us, along with Wloch's daughter, Elga Kruger, and her husband Richard, sit around Wloch's living room and drink tea.

Elga's numerous facial warts accentuate her large nose and buck teeth. Richard always hides his intelligent eyes behind dark glasses that sit on his pointed, blemished face. Their personalities, however, are as friendly and pleasant as their looks are deficient.

'So, what are they importing these days?' Richard asks me. Before the invasion, Richard was a sales representative for the Kiwi Company. He is still well-connected throughout the city. He works with Wloch in the black market.

'Some linoleum, but not much.'

'No need for it,' Wloch says.

'We're also importing quite a bit of linen for shirts and bed-sheets.'

Richard waves his hand. 'I couldn't do anything with that, either. What else?'

I think for a moment. The company hasn't been selling much of anything.

Wloch asks, 'What happened to that consignment of knitting wool we received from E.G. Schmidt just before the invasion?'

Richard leans forward. 'Knitting wool? I know several people who might buy that.'

'It's still in storage,' I say. 'I saw it this afternoon.'

Richard shakes his head. 'If they sold it last winter, it'd be worth its weight in gold.'

I say, 'Janina knows the wool is there, but she doesn't know how to sell it.'

'And since the shipment's on consignment,' Wloch says, 'It's not in the inventory reports. So, there's a good chance the Germans don't know about it. That would explain why they haven't confiscated it for the army.'

Richard rubs his hands together. 'How much is there?'

'At least a truckload.'

Richard flashes a broad grin of yellow teeth. 'Sounding better and better. If we're going to arrange a transaction, Janina will have to be involved. Do you think she'd be interested? For a percentage of the profits, of course.'

'How would it work?'

'The Nazis have set official prices for everything at about a fourth of what the market is willing to pay. So, I find a buyer who pays us the market price. We pay the company the official price and split the difference.'

'If the Nazis don't know about the wool, why give the company any of the money?'

'By showing the sale on the company's books, it appears legitimate and reduces our risk of getting caught.'

'How much would Janina get?'

'A third. You'd get a third, and we'd get a third. Does that sound fair?'

Three months later, I sit at my desk trying to avoid dripping sweat on my correspondence. The weather is still unusually hot and muggy. Janina agreed to participate in the wool deal, but needed a larger percentage of the profits to cover the necessary bribes in the Trustees' office. Richard and I agreed. Due to the balmy weather, however, Richard could only find a buyer willing to pay three times the wool's official price, but still leaving significant profits to share. Janina has arranged for the wool to be picked up today by a division of the German Army. I can't believe it. German soldiers will be delivering the wool directly to Richard's buyer.

At the hottest part of the day's heat, I hear heavy footsteps on the stairs at the end of the hallway. My pulse races. A moment later, two soldiers approach my desk.

'We're here to pick up a shipment of wool,' the taller of the two says in German. His piercing dark eyes stare at me from beneath a shiny black helmet.

'Follow me,' I say with as much nonchalance as I can muster. I lead them to the storage room. I had removed my personal belongings weeks earlier. I open the door and show them the wool. Sweat drips down my sides under my shirt.

'Jesus Christ!' the shorter one says, 'this will take hours.'

I had spent months thinking about how best to move the wool. 'If you pull your truck under the window, you could drop the boxes directly into it.' Acid churns in my stomach.

The taller one nods. 'Bring the truck round.'

During the hour it takes them to remove the wool, I can't get any work done. I worry endlessly that something might go wrong. Janina will be paying part of the additional bribe money to the garrison commandant. Can he be trusted? I wipe my hands on the legs of my trousers. The commandant is in the German Army. The same army that swept across Holland, Belgium and France two months ago. And he's a Nazi – a Nazi who has agreed to accept a bribe. Of course he can't be trusted.

I wipe the sweat from my face. The churning in my stomach becomes more violent. When the soldiers finish loading up, I ask them to sign for the wool. After they leave, I present Janina with the receipt. 'You did it,' I say, and collapse in a chair.

'When do we get the money?' she asks, rubbing her blood-shot eyes.

'Richard will deliver it tonight. I'll bring your share tomorrow.'

'Good. I'd like to get this over as soon as possible. I don't think I can do anything like this again, David. I haven't slept in days.'

That night, two hours before curfew, Richard arrives home with a suitcase full of zloty – more money than I've seen in a long time. Wloch, Richard and I raise our wine glasses.

'*L' chaim.*'*

A few days later I walk into the office of the General Trustee for Jewish Property and place a small package on Miss Demske's desk.

'What's this?' She asks.

'Six pairs of silk stockings. I promised to get you some if I had the opportunity.'

She blushes. 'How can I repay your kindness?'

'If I ever need a favour, perhaps you'd be willing to help.'

She flashes me a perfect smile. 'You can be assured that I will.'

In the early morning hours of 3 September, Sophie sits bolt upright in bed. Sweat forms a sheen on her face. She stares across the darkened room, images from her dream still vivid in her mind. She saw David lashed to a tree, ropes cutting into his bloodied wrists. Wild, hairy beasts with glowing blue eyes gnawed at his flesh while he screamed for mercy. The beasts laughed, stood upright, and goose-stepped around him, their arms raised in a Nazi salute.

Gasping for air, Sophie staggers out of bed and sits on a chair in the corner of the room. Her hands tremble as she lights a cigarette. Something terrible is about to happen.

---

*Cheers!

8 Gestapo

Sophie is sitting in a chair in the corner of the room when I wake. 'You're up early,' I say and begin dressing for work. She frowns. 'Are you all right, *Häschen*?'

'Do you have to go to work today?'

'Of course.' I slip into my shirt and fasten the buttons.

'I have this terrible feeling something is about to happen.'

Here she goes again. I pull on my trousers. 'Why are you doing this to yourself?'

'Something's wrong, David. I can feel it.'

I hate it when she does this. 'Feel what?' I slide my feet into my shoes.

'I don't know, but I have this terrible feeling . . .'

'Stop it, Sophie! You and your terrible feelings. We're still together, aren't we? It's been a year now. We still have food. We still have a place to live. Why can't you appreciate the good things in our life?' I storm out of the room, my shoes still untied. After a few bites of bread in the kitchen, I walk into the living room. Sophie is sitting on the couch, the only furniture left in the room.

'I can't help what I feel. I lost my father and my brother. If I lose you . . .'

I don't want to hear anymore. I spin towards her. 'Why must you always be so miserable? What are you afraid of? Are you afraid we're going to lose our apartment? I can't do anything about that. There's a war going on!'

She lights a cigarette and stares at the match flame, tears in her eyes. 'That's not it. I don't care about the apartment. I'm just afraid. Can't you understand that? I woke up this morning with a feeling that something terrible is about to happen to us.'

'Stop saying that!' I point my finger at her. 'You're making yourself crazy. And you're making me crazy. The war is not my fault! What do you want from me?'

'I don't want anything from you. You don't understand.'

'I don't have time for this.' I press the palms of my hands against my temples. After a moment, I relax. 'Listen, Sophie, I have a busy schedule today and probably won't be home until curfew. Try to get some rest.' I kiss her forehead and leave.

Later that morning, Sophie sits at the table watching Micki play with Wanda's blonde braid. Standing behind Wanda's chair, Micki bats the braid over one of Wanda's shoulders, then the other. Whenever Wanda flips it back, Micki giggles.

Suddenly, there is a heavy pounding on the front door.

'I'll get it,' Sophie says, standing up from the table. Crossing the living room, she calls out, 'Who is it?'

An angry voice barks out, 'Gestapo! Open the door!'

The words slam into her. She can't breathe. Her knees buckle. She stops and leans against the back of the couch. What can they want?

More pounding. 'Open up! Now!' She unlocks the door, but before she can turn the handle, the door flies open. Three men in black leather coats burst in and surround her, their dark eyes determined.

'Where is David Götzel?' the tallest one demands. His right eye squints at her.

'He's not here,' she squeaks, her throat tight and dry.

'I didn't ask you where he isn't. Who are you?'

'Sophie Götzel, his wife.'

'Where's your husband?'

'At work.'

'Where is that?'

She gives him the address while the other two snoop around the living room.

'Why doesn't your husband wear an armband?' the squinty-eyed bully asks. One of the other men sticks a knife in the couch and tears it open.

'What are you doing?' She demands and starts toward him. The one with the squint pushes her hard against the wall. Pain shoots up her back. He brings his face next to hers. His eyes are full of hatred. The smell of cigarettes is on his breath. He presses his forearm across her throat. She can't breathe.

Wanda walks out from the kitchen with Micki. 'What's going on here?' He releases his grip on Sophie's throat, and she sinks to the floor.

'Sit over here,' he tells Wanda, 'and don't say anything.' She carries Micki over and joins Sophie on the floor.

He says, 'Your husband should learn to obey the law.' He pulls pictures off the wall, tossing them over his shoulder. They crash to the floor scattering glass shards. For 15 minutes, the three men rip everything out of the closets and drawers and dump them on the floor. They find nothing. One of them picks up the telephone.

'No one is to leave for the next 30 minutes. I'll have a sentry outside with orders to shoot.' With an exaggerated yank, he jerks the phone wires out of the wall and throws the telephone across the room. 'Make no attempt to contact your husband.'

All morning, I have been at my desk dealing with correspondence. At noon, I suddenly hear boots pounding up the stairs. Three men in black leather coats approach my desk – Gestapo. My pulse quickens.

'Where is the Kommissar?' the tallest one demands. His right eye squints at me.

'First door on the right,' I answer. They march into Janina's office without knocking. The door slams shut. My body jumps.

The hallway quiets. I listen closely for any sound. When I hear my name, my head sinks into my shoulders. I look for a place to hide. Maybe I should leave while they're still in there, but if they know where I work, they might know where I live. Maybe I should wait.

The door opens. I peek over my shoulder. Janina steps out of her office, her face deathly pale. Her red puffy eyes stare down at the floor. She wrings a white linen handkerchief as she leads the three men towards my desk. They stare at me. I look back down at my correspondence, but I can't bring anything on my desk into focus. My pulse throbs in my ears. My heart goes into spasms in my chest. My body shudders.

Relax, I tell myself. Everything is going to be all right. I'm imagining it. They didn't mention my name. They aren't staring at me. Their presence here has nothing to do with me at all. They'll walk past my desk and leave. But they stop.

'Are you David Götzel,' asks the same deep voice as before.

I peer up into hate-filled eyes and nod.

'You are under arrest.'

I ask meekly, 'Why?'

'For not wearing a Jewish armband as required by law. You will come with us.'

How did the Gestapo find me out? As I rise to my feet, the room swims away from me. I take a deep breath to steady myself. What will they do to me? What will happen to Sophie and Micki? I have to do something. Anything. How can they know for certain I'm Jewish? I don't look Jewish. I hold my arms out and offer them an innocent smile.

'But I'm not Jewish.'

'You will come with us.' The shortest of the three grabs my arm and pushes me down the hall toward the stairs.

'But there must be some mistake,' I stammer. 'I'm not Jewish.' They ignore my pleading and shove me down the stairs and out of the building. On the street, a black Mercedes waits.

'Get in,' one orders while another opens the rear door.

'But I'm not . . .'

'Now!' They push me in the car, and I find myself seated next to another member of the Gestapo. The one with the squint sandwiches me into the back seat, while the other two climb in the front.

'Give me your papers,' the new one demands, holding out a gloved hand.

I reach into my pocket and hand him my work permit and identification card. 'There must be some mistake,' I try again. 'I'm not Jewish.'

'Sure,' the leader says as he glances over my documents. 'If you're not Jewish, as you claim,' he turns and smiles at me, 'then prove it. Take off your trousers.'

'Excuse me?'

'Remove your trousers. We'll see if you're Jewish.' The two in the back seat grab my arms while the two in the front pull my trousers down to my knees. I close my eyes. This is it. They'll certainly shoot me for lying.

'What kind of man are you?' The leader asks in disgust, releasing his grip.

I open my eyes and look down. The end of my penis is wedged between my legs, hiding my circumcision.

'I can't tell a thing,' he says, 'except that you are pathetically small, *Jude*. Pull up your trousers.'

I take care not to expose myself while I rehitch my trousers. I try talking my way out of it again. 'As I said, I'm not Jewish.'

'You're a lying Jewish pig!' The leader waves his finger in my face. 'And we're going to learn the truth. Let's go to headquarters.'

The car pulls away from the curb. I'm sweating profusely and shivering with cold simultaneously. I'm under arrest and on my way to Gestapo headquarters. My armband, the proof of my crime, is in my pocket. I just denied my faith and my heritage. I just lied to the Gestapo. What is going to happen to me?

Fifteen minutes later, inside Gestapo headquarters, the same four men push me into the basement. The scraping of our soles against the concrete floor fills the silence in the long narrow hallway.

'In here,' the leader commands, opening a heavy door. The man with the squint shoves me into a tiny, dark room. I bump into a small table. Pain radiates from my hip. He clicks on a lamp and turns it toward me. 'We'll see if you're Jewish. Stand over there.' He sits behind the table. 'Now, lower your trousers.'

There will be no hiding my circumcision this time, but I've been thinking of an explanation, a way to defend myself. I drop my trousers, and the leader scoffs, 'You're obviously Jewish, Herr Götzel. You can't deny it now.'

'I had phimosis performed on my penis while I was living in France due to a bad case of venereal disease.' I lower my head. 'I'm not proud of it, but it's the truth.'

He leans forward on his elbows. 'Do you have a medical certificate?'

I shake my head. 'My visa had expired before the surgery.'

The leader stands and begins to unbuckle his belt. 'I grow tired of your denials, Herr Götzel. Turn around and face the wall.'

'Turn around?' I ask. Squint smiles. The leader nods. With my trousers still draped over my shoes, I turn. My stomach twists into tentacles of nausea that twitch in my belly.

'Bend over. Put your hands on the wall.'

What?! As I bent forward, the cheeks of my buttocks separate. The cool air of the room moves across my anus. I feel so vulnerable. My hands shake as I place them against the cold, damp concrete. I've heard rumours of Gestapo homosexuality, horrible rumours.

'Are you Jewish?' The leader asks calmly.

I hear the clink of his belt buckle. 'No,' I say.

A hissing sound is followed by a loud thwack. Intense pain explodes across my bare buttocks as I arch my back and cry out. My knees buckle. I lean heavily against the wall.

'I'll ask you again.' The leader's voice remains calm, 'Are you Jewish?'

I can't change my story now. They'd shoot me for sure. 'No,' I whisper.

Again, I hear the hiss of the belt knifing through the air, hear the slap of the leather against my skin, feel the pain – excruciating, intense. Knees buckle. Vision blurs. Nausea. Dizziness. Images flash through my mind: Sophie sitting at a small wooden table in the Foreign Students' Club in Paris, sharing a bottle of port with me in her apartment, smiling at me on our wedding day, Micki's pink face the first time I held her in my arms.

'Think carefully before you answer again, Herr Götzel. Are you Jewish?'

What can I do? I have to stick with my denial, don't I? 'No,' I whisper.

Hiss. Thwack. Pain. I fall to my knees, press my cheek against the cold wall.

'Why are you doing this to me?'

'We just want the truth, Herr Götzel. Stand up.'

'I can't.'

'Stand him up.' Two sets of rough hands grab my arms and jerk me to my feet.

'Are you Jewish?'

'No.' Thwack. My backside goes numb. The belt feels more like ice than leather.

'Are you Jewish?'

'No.' Thwack. I collapse to my knees again, my body limp.

'Are you Jewish?'

My shoulders heave as I press my face against the wall and cry, 'No, no! I've told you already.' Thwack. White-hot pain explodes higher on my back. I sob uncontrollably.

'You know, Herr Götzel, we'll eventually find out the truth one way or another. Even if we have to research your birth records.' Thwack.

'Please stop. Please, I beg you.'

'And if you make us do all that extra work, your punishment will be much worse. Now, I'm going to ask you once again. Are you Jewish?'

What did he say? The words jumble in my mind. My punishment will be worse if I make them do extra work? What could be worse than death?

'I'm waiting for your answer, Herr Götzel.'

Maybe they aren't planning to kill me. Maybe if I tell them the truth, they'll stop beating me. Maybe they'll allow me to live, if only for a short while.

'Herr Götzel, I need your answer.' His belt buckle clinks.

Maybe the truth is my only hope of ever seeing Sophie and Micki again. If he's going to kill me, he'll do it regardless of what I say. I don't have to die denying my faith.

'Yes,' I mumble. 'I'm Jewish.'

'I believe you're finally telling us the truth, Herr Götzel.' He turns to the other two. 'Clean him up. I'll meet you upstairs.'

After I sign a confession, they escort me back to the black Mercedes. Ten minutes later, painful tears of remorse sting my eyes as I ascend the steps to Mokotow prison and wonder how long it will be before I see my family again. If I see my family again.

As the sun settles in the west, the light in the apartment fades. Sophie and Wanda continue cleaning up the mess left by the Gestapo. By focusing all her energy on the bedroom, Sophie has no strength left with which to talk, think, or worry.

A soft knock on the front door disturbs her concentration. She lets Wanda answer it.

'O Wanda, isn't it awful what happened to David?' It is Elga Kruger's voice.

Sophie hurries into the living room. 'What have you heard?'

'Fräulein Joblanska called us. Your phone isn't working.' She looks around the apartment. 'What happened here?'

'Elga, please! What happened to David?'

'The Gestapo arrested him this afternoon. Richard made some calls. Apparently he's in Mokotow prison, but Richard is still trying to confirm that. He told me to tell you not to worry. David has many friends in the city, and they'll all work to free him. With luck, he should be home tomorrow. Certainly within a few days at most.'

9 Prison

'In here,' the burly guard orders. He leans against the steel bars of the open cell door and points. 'Take any empty bunk.' I limp past, eyes down. I am carrying a dark brown horse blanket that smells of dust and mould. On top of the blanket are a chipped, red enamel bowl and a bent metal spoon.

The holding cell stinks of unwashed bodies, urine, and human excrement. The stench makes my eyes water. As the door clangs shut, my heart jumps. The sound of the heavy metal lock grips my chest. Despair descends upon me.

On the end of a black wire, a bare bulb hangs from the centre of the ceiling, emitting a sickly yellow light. The air inside the cell is stifling. Along the top of the back wall, just below the ceiling, is a narrow horizontal opening divided by vertical bars. It allows some outside air in, but not nearly enough. I remove my suit coat to avoid fainting.

In the cell two dozen unshaven prisoners loiter. Wooden bunks, covered with straw, line the side walls and crowd the centre of the cell. In the rear corner, two men sit on the only toilets. They stare at their trousers bunched around their ankles.

As I study my cellmates, they suddenly turn and glare back. I look away and limp over to an empty bunk. Sitting down, I feel sharp pains from the welts on my buttocks. I fold my coat in my lap and stare at a crack in the floor. What have I done?

A different stench assails me. I look up. An obese mountain of a man with a scruffy beard stands beside me. Without invitation, he settles onto my bunk. The boards creak in protest. He smiles and says, 'Nice suit.' His breath smells worse than his body, and I can't imagine what keeps his corroded teeth anchored in his inflamed gums.

He asks me in Yiddish, '*A jiid?*'*

'Yes, I'm Jewish,' I respond in Polish. I hope he's not planning to hurt me. I doubt any of the others will come to my aid.

'Why are you here?' he asks.

I stare at the floor. 'Not wearing an armband.' I begin to calculate how long it would take a guard to run down the hall and unlock the door after I scream for help. (Would a guard run down the hall to help an inmate?) I calculate how long it would take for a guard to stroll down the hall. I'd be dead before he got here.

'Where are you from?' He asks. His dark, sunken eyes study me. I look toward the cell door. (Where's the guard?) I pretend I didn't hear the question. He pokes me on the shoulder. 'Where are you from?'

'I was born in Germany.' I didn't say Baden-Baden because I don't want to explain where Baden-Baden is. I don't want to talk at all, especially not to this fellow.

He leans over and savagely shoves me off the bunk. 'There's no room here for German Jews!' I land on the concrete floor. Pain shoots up my back. He slaps my blanket, bowl, and spoon off the bunk and walks away. Halfway across the cell, he glares back with murder in his eyes. My body shivers as his eyes bore into me. As quietly as possible, I gather my things and go stand by the door.

A million people live in Warsaw: Poles, Ukrainians, White Russians and Jews. The Poles hate the Ukrainians, the Ukrainians hate the White Russians and the White Russians hate the Jews. The only thing they all have in common is their mutual hatred of the Germans. The Germans, of course, hate everybody who isn't German. Where will it end?

---

*Are you Jewish?

By standing at the door, I hope the guards down the hall will see me occasionally. As long as I keep my gaze trained in their direction, I feel a little safer. Besides, I don't want the other prisoners to see the tears spilling down my cheeks.

Two hours later, a guard walks down the hallway. He has a long, bony face. His head tilts to the side and most of his left ear is missing. If I am going to survive prison, I will need help. When he passes, I whisper, 'Would you like to make some money?'

He stops and looks up and down the hallway. His left ear is a mangled lump of scar tissue. He looks me over. After a moment, he leans toward the cell door, his eyes scanning the area. 'I'll be back later,' he whispers with a subtle nod. I return his nod, and he moves down the hall.

Hours pass before he returns. 'What did you have in mind?' he asks.

'If you'll contact my Kommisar, she'll pay you to help me.'

He removes a pen and small pad of paper from his pocket and hands them to me. 'Write her a note. I'll see what I can do.' I write a quick note to Janina and another to Sophie. He takes them and leaves.

I turn around. The large inmate is sitting across the cell talking to others. His back is to me. The bunk closest to the door is empty. I've been standing for hours, and I'm so tired. I walk towards the bunk, keeping an eye on the mountain. I settle on to the bunk and feel immediate relief. Everyone inside the cell ignores me.

An hour later, the door clangs opens and two guards enter carrying a black kettle.

The prisoners form a line around the cell, and although I'm sitting on the bunk nearest the door, I walk across the cell and stand at the end. My stomach rumbles while I wait for every-one else to be served. When my turn arrives, the first guard ladles a brownish, watery soup into my bowl. The next guard hands me two pieces of dark bread. After serving me, they carry the kettle to the next cell. I sit on my bunk and inspect my first prison meal.

The bread looks fresh, but tastes doughy. The soup is mostly warm broth, and I can find only two small pieces of potato hidden beneath its surface. As I fish around the bowl for other pieces of potato, a sharp blow on the side of my head knocks me sideways.

'I said there's no room here for German Jews,' the familiar voice says. I look up as the huge inmate circles my bunk. He steps forward and gives me a powerful shove that sends me sprawling to the floor. My bread and soup spill across the dirty concrete. He then pitches my blanket in my face.

'Sleep on the floor where filthy German bastards belong.' Before he leaves, he grinds my bread under the heel of his mud-stained boot.

Too afraid to move, I watch his worn heels retreat across the cell, leaving a trail of scattered breadcrumbs in their wake. When he reaches the other side of the cell, his friends laugh. The other inmates turn away. As I chew my only bite of food, the salty taste of blood mixes with the doughy bread.

Another inmate jumps off a bunk. Like a nervous squirrel, he scoops the crumbs from the dirty floor, looks at me, then dashes back to his bunk, stuffing the bread into his mouth.

I retrieve my spoon and bowl, then crawl to the bars next to the door. I keep my back to the other inmates. A dozen cockroaches join me as I lay on my side. My stomach growls. My head hurts. My back aches. My buttocks throb. I've never felt more alone.

After Sophie finished cleaning up the flat, she spent the rest of the evening pacing the apartment while Wanda looked after Micki. Just before curfew, she hears a knock and hurries to the front door. Could David have been released already? She opens the door to find a skinny man with a bony face, wearing a uniform that she doesn't recognize. He hands her a folded slip of paper. As he tilts his head to one side, she notices that most of his left ear is missing.

She unfolds the paper and immediately recognizes David's handwriting.

> Dear Sophie,
>   I'm in prison on Rakowiecka Street. I'm fine. With help, I should be home within a few days.
>   Please contact Janina at work. She'll help. Then contact Fräulein Demske at the office of the Chief German Trustee. She has connections inside the Gestapo.
>   Don't worry, *Häschen*. Everything is going to be all right.
>
>   Your David

She can't believe it. Everything is going to be all right? How can he say that? He's in prison! Tears threaten to spill down her face. At least he's alive. She looks into the stranger's dark eyes for comfort, but finds none.

'How did you get this note?' she asks.

'I work at the prison.' His voice has a nervous edge. It makes her uncomfortable.

'What can you tell me about my husband?'

He shrugs. 'He's in prison.'

'Can you help get him out?'

He shakes his head.

'Why have you come?'

'I expect to be paid.' Typical Polish generosity!

'Will you deliver a note to him for me?'

'For a price.'

The other prisoners gradually settle into their bunks and fall asleep. When the thin guard returns, I rise to my feet and brush the cockroaches off me. He hands me two pieces of paper, which I slip into my pocket.

'I contacted your Kommisar,' he whispers. 'You have power-ful friends. I'll try to get you some different clothes as soon as I can.'

'Clothes aren't what I need.' I press my face between the bars. 'I have to get out of here. They pushed me off the bunk, spilled my food. I haven't eaten since breakfast.'

He raises his index finger to his lips and looks over his shoulder. 'I'll try to get you transferred to solitary.' A cough echoes down the hall. With a start, he leaves.

I remove the papers from my pocket and sit on the floor. They are letters from Sophie and Janina. They both promise to do what they can. I hope they can do enough.

I scrape about the floor for loose straw to make a pillow. The musty smell of the damp straw helps block the stench in the cell. A chorus of snores rises from behind me as I draw the horse blanket around my neck. I roll onto my side and whisper, 'Hear, O Israel: the Lord is our God, the Lord is One. Into Your hands I commend my body and my spirit. Please watch over my family in my absence.'

Before sunrise, I'm awakened by what feels like a pin pricking my side. I scramble to my feet. Against my skin, under the waistband of my trousers, I find a small insect not much larger than a flea. I hold it between my thumb and index finger and study it. A louse. One night in prison and I'm infested with lice. I loathe the filthy parasites. Has this one just infected me with typhus? I roll the pest onto my thumbnail and use my other thumbnail to squash it. After I hear the faint click of its body collapsing, I sit back on the floor and begin the painstaking process of delousing my clothes.

At first light, the other inmates begin to stir. The thin guard returns and points at me from the hallway. 'You there. Get up! What are you doing on the floor?'

Confused, I climb to my feet as he opens the cell door and enters.

'Come here,' he orders, then slaps me across the face. (What is this about?) He walks to a middle bunk. 'This will be your

71

bunk.' He glances menacingly at the other prisoners, then raises his finger at me. 'Don't sleep on the floor again or everyone will be punished.'

I lay my blanket on the bunk. As he leaves, the breakfast kettle arrives.

The breakfast kettle smells the same as the dinner kettle, and the prisoners form the same line around the cell. I move to the rear and wait my turn. This time, however, when I receive my food, I devour it immediately without sitting. I'm not sure if the bread was doughy, and I'm not sure if the soup was potato, but my stomach is full for the first time in 24 hours: slightly unsettled, but full none the less.

Sophie hardly slept last night. The image of David being tortured in some dark prison cell prevented it. She feels she has to do something to help her husband, and she has to do it today. Using the neighbour's phone, she calls Janina. Although unavailable until after lunch, Janina promises to help her find a lawyer. When she calls the office of the Chief German Trustee, they tell her Miss Demske is ill and in the hospital in Mokotow.

An hour later, Sophie arrives at the hospital to visit Miss Demske. The hallway is full of Germans. Sophie tugs at her black fur cape, pulling it lower over her armband. The nurse behind the counter looks up as she approaches. 'I'm looking for Fräulein Demske.'

The nurse points to a small waiting room. 'Have a seat. I'll see if she's available.' The waiting room is empty except for a few chairs pushed against the wall. Sophie tries to make herself comfortable. Before she's settled, another woman enters the room and coughs. The woman is extremely thin. A hint of rouge is the only colour in her ashen face. She stares at Sophie through dark circles that shadow sunken eyes. 'You wanted to see me?' she says.

'Fräulein Demske, I am Sophie Götzel. I understand you know my husband, David.'

Demske nods. 'His arrest was most unfortunate.'

Despite the physical effects of her illness, her beauty shows through, and Sophie wonders how this striking woman has come to know her husband. But now is not the time to ask. 'Do you think you could help us?'

Demske coughs – a deep, mucous cough. 'I don't know. I have a friend in the Gestapo.' She stands and coughs again. Sophie holds her arm, and they walk toward the doorway. 'I'll ask him if he can do anything for your husband.'

Sophie squeezes Demske's arm. 'Thank you.'

Demske puts her arm around Sophie. 'I'll call you in a couple of days. I should know something by then.' She then leans closer and whispers, 'If we should meet again, it would be better for us both if you don't wear this.' She taps Sophie's armband.

The rest of the day is a blur. Janina and Sophie spend the afternoon visiting one lawyer after another. One refuses to work for Jews. Another won't work for Germans. Another can't appear before a Nazi court. Nothing seems real.

By dinnertime, she is sitting in the tiny office of a lawyer who has agreed to help. He drafts a petition which they need to file downtown before sunset. But if the lawyer holds any hope for David's release, he isn't sharing it with them.

10 Solitary Confinement

In the ensuing days I try to be as inconspicuous as possible. Most of the time I sit on my bunk and search quietly for lice. I try to avoid eye-contact with the other inmates, and speak only when someone speaks to me. When I do speak, I keep my answers brief. During at least one meal each day, the large inmate slaps me, pushes me, or knocks my food to the floor. He takes great joy in my torment.

At the end of the week, two guards I have never seen before escort me to the Gestapo headquarters. Inside a small room I stand before a long desk. Two stony-faced officials look over paperwork while a third takes notes.

'David Götzel, you were caught not wearing a Jewish armband, as required by law.'

I hope a bribe might help. 'I'd like to avoid returning to prison. Perhaps if I pay 3,000 zloty, or its equivalent in gold, we could resolve this minor transgression?' The officials glance at each other. Their chiselled faces disclose nothing.

'You will be advised of our decision.' The guards return me to my cell.

The following week, one of the two guards returns and hands me a sheet of paper. I look at the large black swastika centred below the name of Hans Frank, General Governor for the German Government of Occupied Poland. The typed message reads,

In the name of the German People, I hereby sentence you to eight months imprisonment for not wearing the Jewish star band.

This can't be right. I look up, but the guard has gone. 'There must be some mistake!' The sound of my voice echoes down the empty hallway. *'Eight months?'*

'Eight months?' Sophie paces across the lawyer's office. 'It must be a mistake.'

The light on the lawyer's desk flickers, and a stale cloud of cigar smoke shrouds the top of his bald head. Rain slaps against the window behind him. He leans back in his oversized chair. 'I am sorry Mrs Götzel. It is not a mistake.' He speaks as if her presence is an imposition on his busy daily schedule.

'But he was only arrested for . . .' She collapses into a chair and stares at the floor '. . . for not wearing an armband.' She cannot see because of the tears.

On Saturday, before dawn, the thin guard wakes me. 'This package is from Panienka* Demske,' he whispers, slipping a small parcel under my blanket. After a quick glance over his shoulder, he adds, 'It's all arranged. I'll move you to solitary tomorrow.' After he leaves, I look inside the package and find a fresh loaf of bread and two sausages. I devour them before the other inmates wake.

That night, I hear a commotion. Six black-coated Gestapo stagger down the hallway and stop at the holding cell. They peer in while passing near-empty vodka bottles back and forth amongst each other. The inmates stir restlessly. The mountainous inmate slinks towards the rear wall.

'Open the door,' one of the Gestapo slurs. A guard appears and unlocks the cell. 'Now leave us.' They enter the cell, and

---

*Miss.

the leader says to his comrades, 'We're going to have some fun tonight.' They laugh. 'All Jews, move to the back.' I slip behind the other inmates and stand next to the mountain.

'You,' the Gestapo officer says, pointing in my direction. My knees go weak. 'Yes, you, fat boy,' the officer commands, 'Come here.' The mountain shuffles forward, his head down. The German turns to his comrades. 'He's a nice looking cow, *Ja*?' Their laughter fills the room as the other five Gestapo single out prisoners of their own.

'Now, everyone turn around,' the leader orders. They begin to unbuckle their belts.

Perspiration beads on my forehead as I prepare myself for another beating.

'Everyone, lower your trousers and bend over.'

Once again, I feel the cool air against my bare buttocks. While I wait for the slap of the first belt, the voice of the large inmate cries out. Cries from other inmates soon join his. Above their cries, the sound of the Germans' laughter and taunting banter rises. Under my arm, I steal a glimpse behind me. I turn back around immediately. My entire body shakes as I focus all my attention on the back of my hand. Tears fill my eyes as I study every wrinkle and underlying blue vein. So the rumours of Gestapo homosexual rape are true.

After ravaging a few prisoners each, they remove their belts and beat a few more. They haven't touched any of us along the back wall when they tire of their fun and leave.

The prisoners avoid looking at each other as they quietly settle onto their bunks.

The next morning, the thin guard leads me to a tiny cell in the basement. It is cold and smells of mildew and urine. A single bed occupies half the floor space. From the dim overhead light, a small sink in the corner casts a faint shadow over the stained toilet. The guard points to a large package on the bed: 'Your wife brought that for you,' he says. Then he looks at me: 'No one will bother you down here.'

'How can I thank you?'

'Be sure I continue to be paid.' Before leaving, he hands me a pen and paper.

As the cell door clangs shut, I step over to the sink and pick up a beige block of soap. When I turn the faucet handle, icy water flows onto my hands. I scrub them, then my face. I bounce onto the bed to inspect my package. I feel safe, and with that feeling of safety, a giddy happiness sweeps over me. I am going to survive prison and rejoin my family.

Inside the package I find two clean blankets, a fresh set of clothing, a loaf of bread, six sausages and three letters. I read the letters, then set the clothes out on the cot. Before changing, I wash the rest of my body.

Sophie stands in a queue for over an hour outside the prison. If today is like every other day, she'll reach the front gate in another 30 minutes. Yesterday was Yom Kippur. Has David's fate been sealed inside these walls? Can he feel her presence? She's here, just outside. Is he close? She holds a small parcel containing bread, margarine, sausage – and a letter. Hundreds of others stand in line with her. No one talks. The blistering sun bakes them all. She is afraid that the bread will go mouldy, the margarine melt, or the sausage spoil. But she can do nothing about it. She waits, shuffles forward, then waits again.

When she reaches the front of the queue, she walks through the gate towards the small room where the guards will allow her to leave David's parcel. Before she enters, she glances into the courtyard. Dozens of prisoners, each wearing a pale yellow uniform, walk round the perimeter. She holds her breath. Is her David there? As usual, he's not.

Inside the room, she repeats the daily ritual. She writes David's name and address on the wide ledger page, signs it, and hands them the parcel. The Germans are so efficient, so formal: everything is documented. She leaves through a door on the opposite side.

As she steps out from the shadows of the prison's interior, the strong sunlight stings her eyes. In the letters the one-eared guard sells her every week, David says the extra food is keeping him healthy. She wonders if he is allowed to write the truth. Or do they force the prisoners to write letters as a way of extorting money from their loved ones?

She places her hands against the rough brick wall and looks up at a second-storey window, imagining David behind it. 'Be safe, my love. I'll return tomorrow.'

Back home, Wanda greets her with tears and the latest German decree. Due to spreading typhus, the authorities are setting up a separate Jewish district. Micki and Sophie will have to reside within its boundaries by the first of November. Because Wanda is Catholic, she won't be allowed to go with them.

'What will happen to us?' Wanda asks through her tears. They hold each other. Sophie knows they have little time left together, and yet she finds no comfort in Wanda's arms. She knows comfort is there – she has felt it many times in the past – but she can't feel it now. She can't feel anything.

The happiness of solitary confinement lasted only a short time. All my life I've been active and productive. In solitary, I struggle with the mental challenges of inactivity and confinement.

During my first day in the new cell, I washed, organized my belongings, scrubbed the cell, wrote letters to Sophie, Janina and Fräulein Demske, and ate. That done, I sat and waited for the day to end. The following day, I washed again, ate, wrote more letters, and then waited for that day to end. Each day since has been a copy of the one before.

I pace the length of the tiny cell: four small steps in each direction. I think about Sophie and our life together in Paris. I wonder if she has enough money to buy food for seven more months. How much of Micki's life will I miss? I recite lines from my favourite collection of love poems, Goethe's *Sesenheimer*

Lieder. I try to remember every line of Rainer Maria Rilke's poem, 'Letters to a Young Woman'.

When not reciting poetry, I listen to folk-songs, concertos and symphonies in my mind. Beethoven's fifth has become my favourite. I play it over and over as I pace:

Ta ta ta - TON. Ta ta ta - TON. Ta-ta-ta-ta, ta-ta-ta-ta, ta-ta-ta-ta . . .

Sophie is lying in bed, buried under blankets, drenched in her own sweat, freezing. Panic consumes her. With only a few days left before November, she has yet to find a suitable place for her and Micki to live inside the Jewish district. She is sure the Nazis want to kill her. And she feels so alone, even when talking to other people.

She tried to be strong – she did – but it's too hard. All day yesterday she searched the Jewish district for a place to live. One apartment had no kitchen. How can she care for a child without a kitchen? Another had no toilet. Unbelievable.

And the Nazis haven't yet fixed the boundaries of the ghetto. From day to day they change their minds. She has heard stories of people arriving at their new homes only to find the buildings are no longer within the district. She couldn't cope with that. So, she has focused her search on the interior sections, but those areas are so crowded. Six and eight people sometimes share a single room, and the rents are ridiculously high.

She hasn't yet told David about it. He doesn't need the added frustration of not being able to solve her problems. Since the prison is located outside the ghetto, she won't be able to deliver his packages after they move. What will happen to him then?

Oh God, what is she going to do? She huddles deeper under the covers.

Earlier that morning, Elga Kruger invited her over for a visit. Perhaps she'll go and see Elga this afternoon, if she can find the strength. Elga is one of the lucky ones. Her apartment is already inside the ghetto, so they won't have to move.

From outside her blanket hiding-place, she hears Micki cry. Micki wants her mama. How can she tell little Micki that her mama is here, but not really? She has to return. She has to be strong. Micki needs her. She's already failed David. She can't fail Micki, too.

Climbing out from the safety of her blankets, she calls, 'I'm coming, little one. Mama's coming.' As she walks down the hall to Micki's room, she wonders why Elga wants to see her. Perhaps she knows of an available apartment. She must visit her and find out.

That afternoon, Elga says to Sophie, 'What else can we do?' Her voice is as rough as the warts on her face, but her smile is soft and inviting. 'We have to help each other in times like these.' Tears fill Sophie's eyes. She can't believe what Elga is proposing. 'Sophie, are you all right?' Elga places her arm around Sophie's shoulder. Sophie nods. The swelling in her throat prevents her from talking. 'It's settled then. You'll move in with us.'

I slouch on the floor of my cell with my back against one wall and my bare feet pressed against the cool, rough concrete of the other. If I press hard enough against the walls, I can keep them from pressing against me.

Month after solitary month, Dobry, the one-eared guard, has kept me abreast of the events outside the prison. I eagerly anticipate each of his visits.

The Krugers have welcomed Sophie and Micki into their home, and for that I shall be eternally grateful. By the end of November, the Nazis completed the construction of a wall surrounding the Jewish district. I can imagine the soldiers standing outside the gates of the enclosed ghetto, my family imprisoned inside. Sophie can't bring me packages anymore. Before moving, she entrusted that chore to Janina, along with most of our money.

Last month, just a few weeks after the arrival of spring, 60 prisoners were in the holding cell upstairs when typhus broke out. Forty-five died. Last week the Gestapo transferred most of the survivors to a new prison camp in southeastern Poland. Dobry told me the new prison is located just outside the town of Auschwitz.

With less than a month remaining on my sentence, I pray they leave me here. I'll gladly sit quietly on the floor for the next few weeks and await my release.

11 The Ghetto

By 5 May 1941, I have been in prison for over eight months. Although I completed my sentence on Saturday, Dobry told me I had to wait until today, Monday, to be released. All afternoon, I have been pacing across the confines of my cell like a caged cougar. Where's Dobry? I pace four small steps in one direction. Has something gone wrong? I turn and pace four small steps back. What's the delay? Where is he? I've suffered eight months of inactivity, and Sophie's almost out of money. I have to get back to work. Where is he?

He arrives after dinner and hands me a small sheet of paper: a memorandum from the Jewish department of the Gestapo. It says I am released from prison after serving eight months for not wearing an armband. I shove it in my pocket. 'Can we go now?' He hands me a new armband with a freshly printed blue star. I slip it on and position it above my right elbow. He leads me out of the prison.

I descend the steps of the main gate and breathe deep the sweet smell of spring. Out in the street there is a black carriage waiting. I can see a familiar blonde head in the side window. Janina swings open the door and I climb in. The driver cracks his whip.

'How are you,' she asks.

'Fine. How's my family?'

'They're doing the best they can.' She frowns and looks away.

An uneasy silence settles into the compartment. What does

she mean by that? It doesn't matter. I'll see them soon, and all my questions will be answered. I look out at the street and feel a broad smile spread across my face. I wish the driver would hurry.

As we near the Jewish district, my thoughts wander back to Janina. She cared for and supported us throughout my imprisonment. I take her hands in mine and look into her kind brown eyes: 'I don't know how to thank you for all you've done for my family, Janina, but I promise I'll repay you for your kindness.'

She pats my hand. 'Don't worry about it.'

'Can I work for you again?'

She shakes her head. 'There's nothing more I can do.' The buggy slows to a halt.

As I climb out, I notice a tear on her cheek. 'Good luck, David. Take care of yourself and your family.' The driver's whip cracks, and the buggy pulls away. She kisses her fingers and waves.

'I will, Janina. Thank you.' Tears fill my eyes as I wave good-bye.

Across the street, a wooden railroad gate blocks the narrow opening in a three-metre-high brick wall that stretches as far as I can see in both directions. As I cross the street, a German soldier exits from a small booth. He glances at my sleeve and lowers his rifle.

'*Halt, Jude.* What are you doing out here?'

I stop in the middle of the street. 'I have just been released from prison,' I say, putting my hand into my pocket to get my release paper. The sudden movement startles the guard. He raises his rifle and aims it at my chest, his finger on the trigger. I freeze.

'Wait.' I point with my free hand. 'My release paper is here in my pocket.'

He motions me forward, but the barrel of his rifle remains pointed at my chest, and his finger remains pressed against the trigger. I move forward, my knees quivering. Slowly, I remove the paper from my pocket and extend it towards him. At the sight of the paper, he lowers the rifle to my stomach. When I am within his grasp, he pokes the barrel into my stomach and snaps the document from my hand.

'Prison?' He mumbles, looking at the paper. 'A good place for *Jüden*.' He raises the gate. I force my shaking legs to carry me inside.

The chaos of Leszno Street stops me. Jews are jammed everywhere. Some stand in groups and talk while others push themselves around them. Some lie motionless on the pavement while others step over them. Gone is the sweet scent of spring, replaced by the smell of overcrowded humanity. Here and there I notice men wearing dark blue uniforms. The faces under the caps appear to be Jewish, but their demeanour reminds me of prison guards. I shake off the thought and move into the crowd, eager to see my family.

For two blocks, I muscle my way through people. As I near the iron gate of the Krugers' apartment building, the crowd thins and my pace quickens. I hurry through the first courtyard. Inside the centre courtyard I find the steps I need, and take them two at a time. On reaching the second floor, I knock impatiently at the Krugers' door. When Elga opens it, I throw my arms around her.

'David! What took you so long? We expected you hours ago.'

I don't answer. A beautiful small child with long brown hair stands behind Elga. She looks up at me with large brown eyes, tilts her head to the side, and frowns. She must be at least six centimetres taller than she was eight months ago.

'Papa?' The sound of her sweet voice melts my heart.

'Yes, little one. Papa is home.'

'Papa!' She races toward me. I scoop her off the floor and her tiny arms wrap themselves around my neck, squeezing tears from my eyes.

'I missed you, Micki,' I whisper, holding her tightly to my chest. 'I missed you so much. Did you take good care of Mama while I was gone?'

'David?' Sophie's first utterance comes barely above a whisper. She stands at the entrance to the living room wearing a faded blue housedress. Behind her thick glasses, her wide brown eyes stare at me. I smile, but the tightness in my throat prevents me from saying anything. She runs toward me, throws her arms around my shoulders, and presses her face into my neck. I feel her warm tears on my skin.

'I'm here,' I whisper. 'I'm here. Everything is going to be fine now.'

Later that evening, Richard sits in a chair across the living room from me. He says, 'Whatever your family might need is available inside the Jewish district . . . for a price.'

Sophie and Elga are in the kitchen making tea. I bounce Micki on my knee.

'Of course, we'll have to find you a job of some kind,' he says.

'What's available?'

'Not much.' He looks up at a crack in the ceiling and scratches under his chin. 'The militia are always looking for men, but you wouldn't want to work for them.'

'Militia?'

He looks at me. 'The dark blue uniforms throughout the district. Jewish police. They have replaced the German soldiers inside the ghetto. At first we welcomed the sight of our brothers protecting us. Now, I'm not so sure. They receive preferential treatment and higher rations, and they take their orders from the Gestapo.' He looks back at the ceiling.

'What are you doing to make money?'

He laughs. 'The same thing mostly, I buy and sell. Not much different than before. Second-hand clothing, jewellery, foreign currency. I exchange gold and zloty. Whatever I can get my hands on.' He makes a broad sweeping motion with his arm. 'Most of my old business contacts are locked right here inside the ghetto with us.'

'Is there a way to get outside?' I whisper. He looks at me quizzically. 'If I could contact Miss Demske, she might be able to help me find a job. She works for the Chief Trustee. I've known her for some time. She helped Sophie while I was in prison.'

'The Chief Trustee?' I can see his mind race with thoughts of potential business. Then he shakes his head. 'It's too dangerous. If they catch you outside . . .' His voice trails off. He stands and crosses the room. 'If you're caught outside the ghetto, they won't put you in prison, David. They'll shoot you on the spot.'

'What choice do I have, join the militia? If there's a way over the wall, tell me.'

'Well, you don't have to go *over* the wall.'

Three days later, with a newspaper tucked under my arm, I approach the old redbrick courthouse on Leszno Street. The afternoon sun glares off the walls that extend out from both sides of the building, dividing the Aryan and Jewish sections of Warsaw. I walk past the main entrance. Richard said the courthouse is no longer in official use, and the large iron doors are always locked. Along the side of the building, however, is a single wooden door. I test the handle. It's unlocked, just as he said it would be. I glance over my shoulder, open the door, and slip inside.

A hallway leads me to a large open hall. Like an ancient cathedral, the ceiling arches up from the marble floor to 15 metres overhead. Jews and Aryans fill the dusty, crowded room. They huddle in small groups and talk in hushed tones. As I walk into the crowd, I slip off my armband and shove it into my pocket. On the left side of the hall, I find the stairs Richard described. As I descend into the basement, the temperature drops. At the bottom, I follow a dark hallway to the stairs at the far side.

The Aryan side of the building is a duplicate of the ghetto side. Another open hall leads me past double iron doors to a single wooden door. Richard warned me that the most dangerous part of this journey would be exiting the courthouse on the Aryan side.

The Nazis will pay anyone to turn in escaped Jews, and they pay well.

I take a deep breath, push the door open, and step out into blinding sunlight. As my eyes adjust to the brightness, I scan the street for any sign of danger. Traffic on the street is light. Two Gentiles stroll away from me on the sidewalk talking to each other. They don't appear to notice me. I cross the street and walk down the far side. At the corner, I glance over my shoulder. No one has paid any attention to me.

Two blocks from the courthouse, I try to relax while waiting for the tram that will take me to the Trustee's office. My foot taps the concrete incessantly, and I can't get it to stop. I have been out of prison for less than a week, and here I stand on a street corner violating the same law that landed me in prison. Richard's words ring in my ears: *'If you're caught outside the ghetto, they won't put you in prison. They'll shoot you on the spot.'*

Blood pounds in my head. I can't remember any tram taking this long to arrive. An elderly woman standing next to me smiles and asks for the time. Too afraid to speak, I raise his sleeve and show her my bare wrist. She gives me a sideways look. I smile sheepishly. Does she suspect? I open my newspaper and hide behind it.

When I make it to the outer office where I first met Miss Demske, a receptionist sits at what used to be her desk. She greets me with a curt smile.

'My name is David Götzel, I'm here to see Fräulein Demske, please.' (Does she still work here? I hadn't tried calling her, which was stupid.)

'Do you have an appointment?' I shake my head. She frowns and motions to the waiting area before walking out of the office. I sit down and cover my face with my newspaper. Is the secretary going to get Demske or the Gestapo? I don't have to wait long to find out.

'David, I'm so glad to see you again.'

The sound of Demske's voice brings a smile to my face. She leads me down a hallway and into her office, closing the door. 'It's dangerous for you to be here,' she whispers.

'I had to see you. I need work, and I hoped you could help.'

'I don't know what I can do, but perhaps Herr Eisner could help.'

A few days later, Fräulein Demske sends word for me to visit Herr Schmitz at the Administration of Jewish Property inside the Jewish district.

When I get there and knock, a deep voice calls, 'Come in.' I enter the dimly lit room. A tall slender man with short dark hair stands over a desk covered with papers. I wonder if this is the wrong address. This man is wearing a long dark leather overcoat, just like the Gestapo. As my eyes adjust to the poor light, however, I realize his coat is brown, rather than black.

'Panie Schmitz,' I say. He looks to be in his mid-forties. 'My name is David Götzel. Panie Eisner asked that I speak to you about a job.'

Schmitz nods. 'I was told to expect you. Have a seat.'

I sit on a small chair while he arranges papers on his desk. The dusty office used to be an apartment living room. Against one wall is a worn leather couch. Against the other is a beautiful dark wood china cabinet. The former residents probably left them behind when they made their hasty departure. If only my foresight had been as clear. Two desks sit in front of the only windows. When Schmitz bends forward, his coat opens and I see a German Luger sticking out of his waistband. I'll have to be careful in my dealings with Herr Schmitz.

'I'm the Area Supervisor for the Jewish Trustee,' he says finally. 'As you can see, I have more paperwork than I can handle. I'm responsible for all the buildings in this area of the Jewish district, collecting rents, evicting freeloaders, finding new tenants, and coordinating repairs.' He sits back in his chair and smiles. 'I could use some help.'

'I'd be happy to do whatever I can.'

'Good. The position pays a small salary, and you can take the next vacant apartment for your family.' He sifts through his stack of papers. 'Here's a list of all the apartments and shops and their monthly rents. The janitors will show you all the necessary repairs. After you have visited each building, prepare a report for my review. Have it done by the end of the month. When the first of June arrives, you'll be too busy collecting rents to finish it.'

12 Loss

Four months later, I'm sitting at my desk searching for the right words to ask my boss for a pay rise. On the first of October, Sophie's mother fainted while standing in line for bread. When she fell, she broke a bone in her foot and hasn't been able to walk since. In order to care for her, we moved her into our room in the Krugers' apartment.

Although Schmitz promised me an apartment, thousands of Jews arrive every month, deported from other areas of German-occupied Europe. Despite the ghetto's rising death toll from exposure, starvation, overcrowding and disease, there are no available apartments. The Nazis force new arrivals into the ghetto faster than existing inhabitants die. Half a million Jews now occupy the six square kilometres of the ghetto – double its population before the war.

'I'm sorry to bother you, Panie Schmitz, but the doctor says my mother-in-law needs bed-rest . . .' The sun glares off the window behind Schmitz's desk, cloaking his face in shadow. 'I can't afford to care for her without an increase in my current salary.'

'I'm sorry, too, Panie Götzel, but I can't pay you any more.' Dejected, I return to my work. I'll have to find another way to earn extra money.

'Starting tomorrow,' Schmitz says later, 'I'd like you to make the bank deposits every Tuesday and Friday. I'll give you a pass so you can leave the district and use the tram.'

The next morning, I use Schmitz's pass to leave the ghetto

and take the tram downtown. While I ride, I'm preoccupied with what I might do to make more money. I glance up at a poster plastered on the inside of the compartment. It has a picture of a sparkling new razor blade and urges everyone to try one today. I don't see any income opportunities for me in the razor industry.

Another poster catches my eye. It depicts a young and beautiful Polish girl offering a loaf of bread to a hook-nosed Jew whose shadow forms the silhouette of the devil. Below the drawing is the warning: *Whoever helps a Jew helps Satan*. The poster next to it simply states: *Jews = Lice = Typhus*. I clench my jaw. If only those responsible for such obscenity had to endure the kind of bigotry they spread!

I notice the other passengers staring at my armband. Whenever I make eye-contact, they sneer. Someone walks by and smacks me on the ear with their elbow. The blow knocks me against the window, bringing tears to my eyes. I look back to see who hit me. An older man sitting across the aisle spits and says, 'Filthy Jew'. I sit close to the window and stare out at the street for the rest of the ride.

Later, as I walk along the downtown streets towards the bank, Polish policemen and German soldiers repeatedly stop me and demand to see my papers. I'm emotionally drained by the time I arrive at the Trustee's bank, where I stand in line and wait for a cashier. To avoid the necessity of explaining my presence, I hold the deposit money openly in my hand for everyone to see. When my turn comes, the cashier I approach looks down at my armband. When he looks up, he surprises me with a smile.

'Good afternoon,' he says as I push my deposit through the cage.

'Good afternoon,' I reply, returning his smile. He is a short Polish man in his mid-forties, with a small wrinkled face. He smiles at me again as he hands me my receipt.

That Friday, I make sure I give my deposit to the same cashier. When he reaches through the cage for the money, he leans closer and whispers, 'Next time, if you come just before closing, we could talk afterwards.'

The following Tuesday, I arrive at the bank just before closing and hand my deposit to the same cashier. When he hands me the receipt, he says, 'Meet me by the gate in the back. I'll be there in a few minutes.' I nod.

Uncomfortable with the idea of loitering behind the bank, I walk down the far side of the street, cross at the corner, and walk back, always keeping the gate in sight. As I near it on my return, the cashier exits and waves. 'Let's go to a place I know,' he says.

'I have to be back inside the Jewish district before eight o'clock.'

'That won't be a problem.' He hesitates, glances about the street, then whispers, 'You'll have to remove your armband before we get there.'

An icy wave of foreboding sweeps over me. But I have to find out what this man wants. I survey the street and slip off my armband. My heart pounds against my chest while I follow him to a small café. As we sit, my stomach rumbles in response to the hearty aroma of cooked potatoes and sausage. He orders a small bottle of vodka and two glasses. Red and white checked tablecloths cover ten empty tables. The plastic smell of the table-cloths reminds me of Sophie's favourite restaurant in Paris.

After the waiter leaves, the cashier asks, 'How are things inside the Jewish district?'

'Difficult. It's hard to make a living.'

He nods. 'It's difficult for me as well. The Germans don't pay much.' The vodka arrives, and he empties the small bottle into our glasses. 'My name is Franciszek Wroblinski.' He tips his glass toward me, then takes a long drink.

I raise my glass: 'David Götzel.' The vodka stings my throat, but its comforting warmth radiates from my empty stomach. I relax in my chair, no longer hungry.

'David,' he says with a warm smile, 'please call me Franc.'

He takes another drink. When he sets down his half-empty glass, he says, 'Perhaps we could help each other.'

I take another drink before I reply, 'What do you have in mind?'

'Well, if you need to buy or sell anything on the Polish side, you could do it through me. I have connections. We could make a little money.'

I want to jump across the table and hug this little man, but can I trust him? I should check with Richard before agreeing to anything. 'I'll have to think about it.'

He finishes his drink, stands, and extends his hand. 'Let me know.'

On Friday, when I walk into the bank, I'm carrying four gold rings, an emerald necklace and two diamond bracelets, all wrapped inside a handkerchief in my pocket.

'I've something to sell,' I whisper to Franc as I pass him my deposit.

'Wait for me at the café.'

By the time he arrives, I'm waiting at a table with two glasses of vodka.

'When I saw that you were a Jew,' he says as he picks up his glass, 'I knew we could do business.' After a drink, he asks, 'What do you have?'

I take the handkerchief from my pocket and slide it across the table. 'These are a few items my associates thought you might be able to sell.' He slips the bundle on to his lap, looks inside, and nods. From my other pocket, I withdraw a small sheet of paper. 'This is a list of the prices we'd like to receive.'

He looks at the paper and smiles. 'This shouldn't be a problem.'

From then on, every time I go to the bank I meet Franc at the café. Over a glass or two of vodka, we exchange jewellery, gold and zloty. He sells the items for whatever he can and pays me the listed prices, keeping any differences for himself. Richard and I split 20 per cent of the listed prices and give the owners of the jewellery the rest. Despite the constant humiliation I suffer on the tram and the downtown streets, I look forward to these meetings. The additional income not only pays for my mother-in-law's food, it also allows me to save a little, and I enjoy Franc's companionship.

In the middle of November I ask him if he could find Wanda for me. At our next meeting, he says Wanda will meet me at the courthouse on Monday, 8 December.

Sophie sits on the couch. She is worried. After two months her mother's foot is no better. The doctor visited this afternoon, but there was little that he could do.

David arrives home and looks around the quiet apartment. 'Where is everyone?'

'Mother's in her room. Everyone else is upstairs visiting with the Koslowskis.'

He sits next to her. 'How is your mother?'

She frowns. 'The same. Always the same. The doctor was more concerned about her malnutrition than her broken foot. He said she won't get better if she doesn't eat. I told him she refuses to eat. I can't even get her to sit up. He just said I had to make her eat. I tried after he left, but she refused. Why must she be so stubborn?'

David kisses her on the temple. 'Let me try.' He stands and walks toward the hall.

'There are grapes on the plate by her bed, and sausage and noodles in the kitchen,' Sophie says.

He turns around. 'I have good news, *Häschen*. I found an apartment.' Not exactly good news to Sophie. Now they'll have to move. 'And Franc has located Wanda. I'm going to see her next month.'

Sophie smiles. 'Can I see her, too?' He nods, and then disappears down the hall toward her mother's room.

A few minutes later, David returns. Something is wrong. He moves slowly across the room, with his shoes scraping the floor as if his feet are too great a burden for his legs to lift. When he sits on the couch next to Sophie, he stares into the distance, his eyes strangely blank.

'I'm so sorry, Sophie,' his voice fades to a whisper. 'Your mother . . .'

'She's dead.' She guesses. He nods and wraps his arms around her.

Now she is an orphan. A great emptiness consumes her. She lost her brother, then her father, and now her mother. Death seems to permeate her existence, claiming everyone she loves. Who will be next? she wonders. But her tears refuse to flow.

She goes to her mother's bedside, her mind numb, her heart like stone. The sunken face on the pillow looks strangely peaceful. Her mother is at rest. She caresses the cold cheek with the back of her hand, and straightens the hair. '*Mutti*,' she whispers, 'I love you, *Mutti*. Sleep well.'

Two days later, in the Cmentarz Zydowski cemetery, Sophie watches them bury her mother in the snow-covered ground. A bitter November wind promises a harsh winter. The cantor sings a haunting song in his beautiful voice. The rabbi prays, 'God, full of mercy, receive this soul and grant it eternal rest.'

Sophie looks at the rabbi. God full of mercy? What kind of God full of mercy allows such things as war, the ghetto, starving children and needless killing? She doesn't understand. Why doesn't He stop the suffering? She would, if she could. Why doesn't He? Her brother, her father, her mother. All dead. Who will be next? The dead no longer feel pain. The dead no longer feel sorrow. The dead no longer feel fear. In a way, she envies them.

During the first week in December, Sophie, David and Micki move into a two-room flat on Chlodna Street. Chlodna Street was one of the last streets added to the ghetto, and their new apartment has two large comfortable rooms. Despite the improved living conditions, loneliness and despair fill Sophie's days. While David works, she shops for food, sews, cooks, cleans and looks after Micki. With sawdust as their only source of cooking fuel, her cleaning is never complete, and the dust makes her lungs ache. She misses the familiar sound of her mother's voice.

On the first Saturday night in their new apartment, with David asleep beside her, she feels restless and overwhelmed. As she lies in bed, she imagines the walls collapsing, crushing her under their terrible weight. Her breathing is laboured, her chest constricted.

For weeks, she's fretted over David's trips to the bank. In early November the Gestapo caught six Jewish women and two Jewish men searching for food on the Aryan side of the ghetto's walls. None of them possessed a pass. On the fourteenth, they were tried and convicted of unauthorized border crossing. Three weeks ago a Nazi firing squad executed them.

Anything could go wrong on David's trips to the bank. What would she do if he's taken away from her again? Her lungs collapse. She can barely breathe. 'David,' she whispers in a panic, clutching her chest. 'David, help me please.'

'What is it, *Häschen*?' He rolls over, still half asleep.

'I don't know,' she cries. 'I can't breathe. The walls are crushing me.'

He wraps his arms around her and gently rocks back and forth. 'You're all right, Sophie. Try to relax. Everything is going to be fine.'

13 Business

Wanda Szcepanska doesn't like crowds. Standing inside the courthouse hall, surrounded by all these people, she feels cornered. If the Germans seal off the Aryan exit, escape into the ghetto will be her only way out – and escaping into the ghetto is no way out.

Three small packages sit at her feet. She has been waiting for the Götzels for 15 minutes. They had better show up soon, or she will have to leave. If she stays in here much longer, she'll go crazy. She hopes the Götzels are all right. When Franc sent word they were alive, the courthouse was the only possible place to meet. But the latest word is that conducting business in here won't be allowed much longer.

She scans the hall again. David's head pokes out from the crowd. She waves. He heads her way. Has it only been 15 months since his arrest? He looks thinner, older.

'David, how are you?' They hug. 'Where are Sophie and Micki?'

He frowns. 'Sophie's not doing well.'

'What's wrong,' she asks as they sit on the floor in the corner.

'Since her mother died, things are just too much for her. She's seeing a doctor today.'

'Sophie's mother?' Wanda places her hand over her mouth. 'When?'

'Two weeks ago.' He explains what happened.

When he finishes, she asks, 'How's Micki?' The sparkle returns to David's eyes.

97

'She's the light in my life.' His soft lips widen into a warm smile. 'When I hear her giggle, feel her arms around my neck, I'm driven to work all the harder.'

If only Wanda could find a husband with half David's devotion. She wraps her arms around his neck. 'Give this to Micki for me.' She kisses him on the cheek, and adds, 'And this to Sophie.' She kisses him on the other cheek.

He asks, 'How have you been?'

'Struggling, but I get by.' She leans forward, 'I'm working with the Underground.'

'The Underground?' He raises his eyebrows. 'Can you get us out of Poland?'

She shakes her head. 'They're too busy with Polish people to help Jews.'

He frowns, then asks, 'Have you heard any news of the war?'

'Haven't you heard? The Japanese bombed an American island yesterday.'

'An American island?'

She nods. 'Some place in the Pacific Ocean. America has declared war on Japan.'

He jumps to his feet. 'That's great news! They'll declare war on Germany, too.' He helps her up, his smile brightening the entire hall. 'The war can't last much longer now.'

'I hope you're right.'

He puts his arm around her. 'You'll see. This will all be over by spring.'

She's heard that before. 'I brought these for you.' She hands him the packages.

'You didn't have to do this.' His cheeks flush.

'There's some rice and bread, potatoes, sausage. Not much, but I hope it helps.'

'How can you afford this?'

'I'm fine. Really.'

'We should do some business together. Franc and I buy and sell things. We can, too.'

'Franc told me. He works with the Underground, too. That's how he found me.'

'Well, I can't carry much to the bank, but you and I could do business here.'

'We'd have to be careful. I've heard the courthouse won't be open much longer.' She dreads the idea of meeting regularly in this place.

'We'll be careful.'

By the time I arrive home that evening, Sophie's already in bed. Her pasty white skin is tinged yellow, and dark rings encircle her eyes.

'What did the doctor have to say,' I ask. She asks me about Wanda, and I tell her our entire conversation before she's willing to talk about the doctor.

'He says I'm run-down, and my nerves are overstrained.' She pulls the covers to her neck. 'I need rest. He says I'm not to cook or clean, and we should hire a housekeeper.'

(A housekeeper? We can't afford a housekeeper, even if Wanda and I start doing business together. Does the doctor know there's a war going on? But if that's what Sophie needs . . .) I squeeze her ankle through the covers. 'I'll look for a housekeeper right away.' And somehow I'll get the money to pay for it. I don't know how, but I'll get it.

A few weeks later, on a cold January evening during the first week of 1942, I knock on the door of a third-floor apartment. The door opens a crack and an apprehensive, bespectacled eye peers out at me. 'Good evening, Panie Reinhardt,' I say. 'I'm here to collect this month's rent.'

The apprehension transforms into welcome: 'Good evening, Panie Götzel. Would you care to come in?' He swings open the door. 'I've a favour to ask of you.' Reinhardt works in the little Schultz factory on Leszno Street as a bookkeeper. He looks like a bookkeeper, too, in his brown suit and gold-rimmed glasses.

'I don't have much time,' I tell him, 'but I can stay for a moment.'

Reinhardt's wife, a short, beautiful woman with dark brown hair and eyes, stands inside the apartment with their two-year-old son leaning against her legs. 'Would you care for some tea?' she asks.

'Please.'

She hurries into the kitchen, their son trailing behind. The smell of boiling potatoes fills the immaculately clean apartment. Reinhardt and I sit at a table in the living room. His brother's four small children stare at me, wide-eyed, from a bed on the other side of the room. The Nazis drove his brother's family out of their home in the country. Two months after arriving in Warsaw, his brother and sister-in-law disappeared. The children, along with another family not related to the Reinhardts, share the small apartment.

I wink, and the children respond with a chorus of giggles. Mrs Reinhardt returns with blue porcelain cups that clink against matching saucers as she sets them on the table.

'I hear you take care of matters.' Reinhardt says, blowing across his steaming cup.

'I do what I can.' I sip the hot, weak tea. It burns my tongue, but the warmth feels good against the January chill. 'What did you have in mind?'

'Before moving here, I buried some diamonds and 20-dollar gold pieces. If you could get them for me, I'd be happy to split them with you.'

I sip more tea. 'How many gold pieces?'

'A hundred.'

'How many diamonds?'

He cups his hand. 'A small bag.'

I nod. This could solve my housekeeper problem.

The next morning I sit at my desk and count yesterday's collections while I wait for Schmitz to arrive. During the eight months I've been here, I've noticed he likes to wear fine clothes, eat in the best restaurants and drink expensive liquor. I'm hoping he might like to make some extra money to pay for it.

He enters with an unusual spring in his step. 'Good morning, Panie Götzel.'

'Good morning, Panie Schmitz. You look to be in a good mood this morning.'

'I am.' He winks. 'I had a good night last night.'

'Doing what?'

He laughs. 'Things family men such as you can only dream about.'

Now feels like a good time to broach the subject. 'I have a business proposition for you. If you'd be interested in making some money.' I watch him. He gives me a quizzical look, gazes down at the money I'm counting, then frowns.

'It has nothing to do with any of the work we do here,' I add quickly.

'Good.' He turns away, leans back in his chair, and stares at the ceiling. In the deafening silence that follows, I return to counting the rents. I guess I'll need to find a different business partner. When I look up, Schmitz is staring at me. 'If your proposition has nothing to do with our work here, I might be interested.' I explain my plan and we agree to split my half of the profits.

For the next two weeks Schmitz and I wait for a storm. After curfew on the first wet night of the year, we approach the ghetto's main gate. We both wear heavy coats, have scarves wrapped up past our chins, and hats pulled low over our eyes. The freezing rain is the perfect excuse to hide our faces. We each carry a briefcase.

Schmitz enters the guardhouse while I wait. I can't stop shivering. The guard shakes his head at Schmitz who takes out a piece of paper and waves it his face. I stamp my feet. Maybe this isn't such a good idea.

A moment later, Schmitz leaves the guardhouse and walks through the gate, motioning me to follow. I hesitate, remembering my last time here with a rifle pointed at my chest. I look at the guard. He waves me through. We're over our first hurdle.

On the Aryan side an enclosed carriage waits for us. As I climb in, Schmitz gives the driver directions across town. In the event of anything happening to Schmitz, I have a pass in my pocket, although I doubt it will do me any good if I'm caught.

I pull my woollen scarf away from my face and look out at the deserted streets. The wind is now blowing the rain sideways. The only sounds I hear are the clip-clop of the horse's hoofs on the wet cobblestones and the steady drum of the rain on the roof of the carriage. As previously agreed, we say nothing. I watch the rain falling, while in my mind I run through Reinhardt's description of the apartment building where he buried his valuables.

When we enter the middle-class neighbourhood of Chmieln Street, I realize that half a block away is the clinic where Micki was born. (Four and a half years ago, I held my daughter for the first time. After the war, I hope Sophie and I will have more children.)

The carriage stops in front of a grey stucco four-storey building. The rain has eased to a steady drizzle. Schmitz tells the driver to wait. As I follow Schmitz to the entrance, I pull my scarf back up under my nose and breathe deep the smell of the wet wool. He tests the front door. It opens, and we enter a darkened stairwell. Besides the pounding in my chest and the chemical smell of some kind of cleansing agent, I sense nothing while we wait for our eyes to adjust to the dark.

Schmitz waves, and we move quietly up the narrow stairs. Halfway to the first landing, we stop and listen again. Nothing. On the second landing we hear footsteps inside an apartment. They sound as if someone is approaching the door. We hurry farther up the steps before stopping and pressing our backs against the wall above the apartment. The footsteps fade. We climb past the third-floor landing.

On the fourth floor, we hear the muffled cry of an infant. When something crunches under Schmitz's foot, we freeze. A woman's voice begins to sing, and the baby's crying stops. We climb on up the stairs and reach the door to the roof.

'Be quick,' Schmitz whispers as he opens the door and hands me his briefcase.

I walk out into the drizzle while Schmitz waits at the door. In front of me, a forgotten sheet hangs heavy on a clothesline. Occasionally, it snaps in the breeze. Beyond the soggy sheet, dark plants and shrubs surround a small white table and four white chairs.

I stay to the left, moving quietly along the edge of the roof toward the chimney. My foot strikes a small stone, and it skitters across the rooftop. The clamour pierces the quiet of the night. I stop and listen. Water drips. The sheet snaps. Nothing else.

I look back at Schmitz who motions me forward.

Next to the chimney is a large circular brick planter, with a small tree growing in the centre. I kneel beside it and set down the briefcases. Opening one, I take out a small shovel. The tree and the chimney are aligned along a north–south axis. I begin digging on the west side of the tree, half a metre from the edge of the planter. The shovel makes a slurping sound in the mud.

Perspiration and drizzle drip from my face. How deep did Reinhardt bury it? The shovel clangs against something. My heart jumps. I push the mud away to find a small metal box. I put it inside the open briefcase, then slop the mud back in the hole, put the shovel in the other briefcase, rinse my hands in a puddle, and walk back to the door.

'I've got it,' I whisper to Schmitz, handing him the briefcase with the shovel in it. 'Let's get out of here.' We start back down the stairs.

As we descend, our steps sound louder to me. My clothes are soaked, heavy with rain and perspiration. Each time I lower myself onto a step, my knees twitch and buckle. I lean heavily against the handrail for support.

Halfway down, a door opens below us, and the first-floor hallway light clicks on. Light filters up the stairway, illuminating the second-floor landing where we stand. I close my eyes, pushing my back into the wall. My body shakes.

The stairway remains quiet. Whoever opened the door is making no sound. Water drips from my hair and runs down my cheeks. I open my eyes. Reinhardt said the lights are on one-minute timers. One minute. Sixty seconds. It can't be much longer.

Slowly, quietly, Schmitz withdraws his Luger from under his coat and holds it aloft. I swallow hard. The light downstairs goes out, but we remain motionless: waiting, listening.

Another minute passes. The door downstairs clicks shut. I look at Schmitz, but can't see his expression in the dark. Now what? Has the person down there gone back inside, or is he still waiting in the hallway? Schmitz motions for me to stay. With his pistol raised and his back against the wall, he glides down the stairs. I peer over the railing. He looks at the landing below and motions for me to follow, putting his pistol away.

We tiptoe down the remaining flight of stairs and out the front door.

'Go,' Schmitz commands the driver as he climbs in the carriage after me.

We pull away from the curb. As I look out the back, I see a heavyset man in trousers and a T-shirt coming out of the building. He stares down the street after us. Schmitz laughs and cuffs me on the shoulder.

Back at the ghetto's entrance, the same guard waves us through the gate without question. We hurry to our office, where I lock the door. Schmitz turns on the desk light and I open my briefcase. He places the muddy metal box on his desk. The small silver key that Reinhardt gave me slips easily into the hole in the box. I turn it. A soft click greets us.

Schmitz opens the lid. Inside are two small grey cotton bags. We each take one and look inside, then laugh. Schmitz tips his out. Dozens of 20-dollar gold pieces clatter on to the desk. I cup my hand and pour, filling it with diamonds. I hold my shaking palm under the desk lamp and watch the diamonds dance and sparkle in the light.

Grinning, Schmitz reaches into his desk drawer and withdraws a bottle of vodka.

An hour later, Reinhardt opens his apartment door. 'Did you get it?'

'We got it,' I tell him.

His wife claps her hands together. 'Thank God you're here,' she says, and kisses me on one cheek while his sister kisses me on the other.

I hand Reinhardt one of the grey bags. 'This is your half.'

He smiles: 'I have many friends with similar needs.'

My nerves twitch. It took half a bottle of vodka to calm down after this trip. Do I want to risk doing it again? But, I did make a lot of money tonight . . . I feel a reluctant smile form on my face. 'I'd be happy to discuss it with them.'

I decide not to tell Sophie about tonight. There is no sense in worrying her. But tomorrow, I'll hire Frau Schrieber as our housekeeper. She is an elderly woman who comes from Sophie's hometown of Wiesbaden in Germany.

Two days later, Frau Schrieber moves into Micki's room and takes over all the household chores. Her cooking is exceptional. She washes clothes until they smell like sunshine. She irons to perfection. And Micki loves her.

With the burden of running the household removed from Sophie, her breathing begins to improve. By the end of her first week, Frau Schrieber is Sophie's new best friend.

Other than an occasional creak and the slight scraping of our feet against the wooden steps, the darkened stairwell remains quiet as Schmitz and I climb. The stale air smells of dust and cigarette smoke. We say nothing to each other.

Every excursion to the Aryan side has been different. Every strategy for retrieval has been unique. Tonight, we'll speak with our client's former neighbour.

Stopping on the third-floor landing, we pause for a moment to collect ourselves. Schmitz nods. I rap on the door and hear a muffled cough from inside the apartment. The door opens and a short man with hairy arms stares out at me. The man wears a stained T-shirt. Hair from his bloated stomach pokes through a frayed hole next to his navel. His hair hasn't seen a comb, nor his face a razor, for at least three days. Black-framed lenses magnify his dark eyes. The smell of mould drifts into the hallway from his cluttered apartment.

He glares over the top of his glasses. 'What do you want?'

I exaggerate my German accent, 'You are Oskar Jelinowicz?'

'*Tak.*'

I point across the hall. 'And the Paul Salzman family used to live there? Correct?'

'Who wants to know?'

I hand him a handwritten note. 'Panie Salzman wishes that you give us the gold pieces he left with you before he moved to the Jewish district.'

The man's eyes cut to Schmitz. 'I don't know what you're talking about.'

I continue, 'Your former neighbour, Paul Salzman, entrusted you with 200 20-dollar gold pieces. He asked us to come here and get them for him.'

'As I said, I don't know what you're talking about.'

I look at Schmitz and nod. 'Perhaps we've made a mistake.' I step back.

As the man begins to shut his door, Schmitz steps forward and blocks it with his foot. 'I'm the German Commissar for the Administration of Jewish Property.' he says. Jelinowicz reopens the door. Schmitz leans in. 'Understand. I will have to open a complete investigation into this matter.' He pulls his coat open and places his hand on his hip.

The man's eyes grow wide as he stares at the German Luger in Schmitz's waistband.

'I think Salzman may have asked my wife to keep a small box

for him. I'd forgotten all about it, and I certainly don't know what's inside. He just asked us to hold it for him. We certainly would have notified the authorities if we knew we were supposed to.'

'You need to give it to us now,' Schmitz states.

The man scurries down the hallway toward the rear of his apartment.

Schmitz glances at me, flashing a devilish grin.

14 Little Schultz

Sophie stands by her open bedroom window and stares out at the humid summer night. It is three o'clock in the morning. The stifling air presses against her flesh. She hasn't slept much this July. Every night, the sheets insist on sticking to her skin, twisting themselves around her body. They'll strangle her if given the chance.

Inside, David's rhythmic snoring fills the room. On the floor in the corner, Micki and Frau Schrieber share a mattress. Two other families also share the apartment. David said it wasn't right for his family to have so much room when so many other families had none.

Looking out the window, Sophie tries not to think about the future. Three storeys below, a dozen Jews sleep on the pavement. The smell of their diseased bodies hangs in the air like an oppressive fog – a constant reminder of death. The dark quiet street beckons. How easy it would be to end her torment. She wouldn't have to jump. If she sat on the window ledge and leant out for air, she might slip. It would be an accident.

The rumble of engines distracts her. Down the street, three vehicles approach. In the front and rear are army trucks, between them a coal-black Mercedes. At the first corner, the truck in the rear stops. Five men wearing the blue uniforms of the Jewish militia climb out and position themselves in a line, blocking the street.

Afraid of being noticed, Sophie leans back inside, but continues to watch.

The Mercedes stops below her window while the first truck proceeds down the street. Exhaust fumes assail her nostrils. The truck stops at the next corner. Five more militia men block that intersection. The doors to the Mercedes open. Four men wearing black leather greatcoats step out. They stand on the sidewalk directly below Sophie and wait.

One of them looks up. She jerks herself back into the bedroom. Have the long knives come for her, or David? Her heart pounds. She tries to swallow against the terror rising inside. Her throat burns. But there is only one way to find out. She peeks out the window. One of them signals, and they cross the street. When they enter the building on the other side, Sophie slumps to the floor in relief. *They haven't come for us – at least not this time.*

She hears shouts from an upstairs window across the street. She looks out again. There is a crash, as if a bureau has been knocked over.

'NO!' Someone cries. Next, a gunshot.

She ducks below the windowsill. Is this really happening? Unable to tear herself away, she uses the curtain to cover half her face and peeks over the sill with one eye. Her body trembles. More yelling. The door opens and the Gestapo drags a grey-haired man from the building. He wears a pale nightshirt and is slumped between two of the men who hold his arms. His bare feet scrape across the cobblestones.

They stuff him in the back seat of the Mercedes and drive to the corner, stopping just long enough to bark something at one of the militia men before disappearing down the street.

The militia waves to the men at the other corner. They all gather in front of the building. Three go inside. A moment later, they carry out the limp body of an old woman. Perhaps she is the man's wife, perhaps his mother – Sophie can't tell. Her attention is riveted on the large black spot in the centre of the woman's nightdress.

Long after the militia men load the woman's body into their truck and leave, Sophie still stares out her window. Stillness has returned to the ghetto night. The exhaust fumes are gone, replaced by the acrid smell of the undisturbed bodies on the sidewalk. There are no truck sounds, no shouting, no gunshots – just David's deep rhythmic snoring.

Did she really witness a murder and kidnapping, or has she imagined it? Self-doubt marches across her mind like the German Army marched into Warsaw. Thump-thump-thump: her head pounds to the rhythm. Images mix with the pounding. Thump-thump-thump (the Nazis trample her father beneath their boot heels). Thump-thump-thump (her brother falls and is gone). Thump-thump-thump (her mother's cheek is cold to the touch).

Tears cascade down Sophie's face and neck, soaking her nightgown.

Wanda scans the crowd in the courthouse for any sign of David. Meeting here isn't safe – hasn't been for months. If it weren't for David, she wouldn't be standing here now. If it weren't for David and Sophie, she corrects herself. David, Sophie and Micki.

Where is he? This meeting will have to be short. She spots him pushing through the crowd. He waves. She smiles and returns his wave. He is a handsome man.

'What took you so long?' She asks. Sweat drips from his brow as she kisses him on the cheek. She tastes his salt on her lips, smells his anxiety.

'I've been fighting my way through the crowd for half an hour.'

'We can't keep meeting here. The Germans are going to close the courthouse soon.'

'Rumours.' He waves his hand. 'There are always rumours.'

'Not this time.' She laces her arm through his and steers him to their corner, where she sets down her heavy rucksack.

'Something's happening. I don't know what, but I've heard unemployed Jews have short futures. I'm afraid. For you, and about meeting here.'

He shakes his head. 'Sophie doesn't have a job, and what about Micki? Children don't have jobs. It doesn't make any sense.'

'I think the Germans are planning something. Listen, if anything happens . . .' She hands him a slip of paper. 'You can reach me at this number.'

He stares at the paper. 'We should find somewhere to hide Sophie and Micki.'

'The SS is paying 500 zloty to anyone reporting a Jew outside the ghetto. For that much money people are turning in their friends. No one would risk hiding a mother and daughter together. If you're caught, you're dead. We'll have to hide them separately.'

'Micki first.' He paces across the corner. 'If she's not going to be with Sophie, she must be somewhere safe, where she'll be taken care of until the war is over.'

'There's a cloister of nuns outside the city who take Jewish girls . . . for a price.'

'Nuns? Would she be safe?'

'I can't vouch for all Catholics, David, but she'd have to be safer with them than here. I do know one thing – it will be expensive.'

'I have money. Set it up as soon as possible. What about Sophie?'

'Adults are more difficult. It will take time.'

'How much time?'

She shrugs. 'I'll do what I can. In the meantime, she should get a job. Is there any other place we could meet?'

'I'll ask around and let you know next week.' He removes his empty rucksack and hands it to her, then lifts hers from the floor and slings it onto his strong, broad shoulders.

She says, 'Last week's jewellery wasn't worth much. I spent most of the money on food. What's left is in here.' She points to a small pocket on the pack's side.

'You should keep it, Wanda.' He removes the pack.

'No.' She stops him. 'This time, you keep it.'

He nods. 'That's the last of the jewellery, anyway. I put gold in there for next week's supplies. Until then . . .' He kisses her hand, turns, and disappears into the crowd.

'I guess I'll see you then,' she whispers after he's gone.

That evening I visit Reinhardt's apartment.

'It's my turn to ask a favour, Panie Reinhardt,' I say as he opens the door.

'Anything for my good friend.' He motions for me to enter.

'I'm worried about my wife,' I begin. 'She has no job, and I've been told that now is not a good time to be without a work-card.'

Reinhardt considers this for a moment before he replies, 'I've heard there's nothing at either big Schultz or Toebbens, but I could get her into the washhouse at little Schultz.'

'I'd appreciate anything you could do.' I shake his hand.

The early morning sun beats on Sophie's back as she trudges down the narrow, crowded street. The ghetto is so crowded now, she can't imagine the Germans forcing any more people into its confines. Like the searing flame of an enormous kiln, the blazing summer sun bakes the ghetto's inhabitants into glazed statuettes.

Sophie's daily trek to work is not particularly long, but neither is it particularly pleasant. As she marches toward the little Schultz factory, she tries not to notice the people sprawled motionless across the pavements. She tries not to wonder if they are still breathing. She tries not to imagine her family lying beside them.

Just report every day, David told her. Frau Schrieber will watch Micki. Sophie is to go in and out of the washhouse and pretend she is employed there. It's all arranged.

If working is so important, what about Frau Schrieber and Micki? she asked him. (He was working on it, was all he said.)

But Sophie can't *pretend* to work, not when so many others go begging for anything that will provide a much cherished work-card, and not when the other women inside the washhouse slave away for ten hours each day, and not when she stands in the same pay line to receive the same few zloty each week, and not when she shares the same coffee each morning and the same bread and soup each afternoon.

By the end of the second day, she began working alongside the others. Every day now she sorts socks, folds linens, sweeps the floor, cleans around the work area – whatever needs to be done. The harder she works, the less she worries about the future.

On Sunday, 19 July, Wanda meets David in the courthouse and gives him the good news, 'The nuns are willing to take Micki.' She leads him to their usual corner. 'Everything is ready. All we need do is get her outside the gate.'

'When?'

'Next month. Tuesday, the fourth.'

'What about Sophie?'

'Nothing so far. Did you get her a job?'

'Last week.'

They discuss the details of Micki's escape, exchange rucksacks, and agree to meet the following weekend.

On Tuesday morning, 22 July 1942, Sophie steps outside to begin her daily trek to work and notices large, bright-yellow posters plastered to the buildings up and down the street. A small group of people stands on the sidewalk in front of the poster attached to her building. She joins them. The poster's large, block-lettered headline calls out:

ATTENTION! ATTENTION! ATTENTION
RESETTLEMENT IN THE EAST

The smaller print says Governor Hans Frank is announcing Jewish employment and housing opportunities available in the Eastern Territories. All unemployed Jewish residents of Warsaw are to report to the railway sidings on the northern edge of the Jewish district. Upon arriving at the *Umschlagplatz*, volunteers will receive twelve kilos of bread and four kilos of marmalade to take on their journey.

Sophie laughs. 'Who do they think will believe this?'

A teenage boy with a dirty face and greasy hair speaks up, 'I might.' Sophie looks down at the dirt-filled scabs on his bruised bare feet. His tattered clothes reek of body odour and urine. Her stomach tightens into a knot.

He says, 'My parents died during the bombing. Typhus took my little sister last week. I sleep on the pavement. I haven't eaten in two days. Housing? Bread and jam? Why not?'

She looks into the haggard faces of the rest of the group. Their heads bob in agreement. Tentacles from the knot in her stomach twitch and pull at her insides. She hurries away, forcing their faces from her mind.

When she arrives at the little Schultz factory, dozens of women wait in line at the entrance. Some carry sewing machines. Others have knitting machines. All seek employment, frightened by what the announced resettlement might mean.

In my office, I stare at Schmitz in disbelief. 'What do you mean, Rolf? Why would Eisner close the office? What about the rent collections and the bank deposits?'

'All Eisner's resources are being shifted from housing to the resettlement.'

'What about my staff? I have 12 people out there.'

'Eisner sent this letter with the notification.' He hands it to me. 'It says you, your family, and your staff are not to be resettled. We'll issue everyone with temporary work-cards, but I think you should find yourselves permanent employment . . . and quickly.'

I pace across the office. All my income sources have vanished. The Germans sealed the courthouse last week, so I can't trade with Wanda for food and supplies. I'll be making no further bank deposits, so, I've lost my business with Franc. The office is closing, so Rolf and I will no longer be able to retrieve valuables on the Aryan side. I try to work out how much gold I will have after paying the nuns to hide Micki. But even with the diamonds I set aside, I doubt we have enough to last us until the end of the war – whenever that will be.

That afternoon, I watch with dismay from our second-storey office window as the first Jewish volunteers file up Leszno Street towards the *Umschlagplatz*. Most wear rucksacks stuffed with belongings, or struggle under the weight of bundles in their arms. Despite the sweltering heat, their bodies look fat from the multiple layers of clothing they wear beneath their winter coats. Many without coats have blankets wrapped around themselves. Many others, more destitute, wear little and carry nothing. Some are old, some are young, some feeble, some healthy. All are unemployed – and all are desperate.

I clench my teeth and beat my fist against the side of my leg in a slow rhythm. Grandparents, parents and children march towards the promise of housing and employment. Their journey to that life will supposedly begin with bread and marmalade. All they need do is report to the railway sidings at the northern edge of the ghetto . . . What is really going to happen to them? I don't believe the posters, and I doubt if the Jews filing past me on the street below believe them either. Their willingness to embrace this ruse must result from desperation not gullibility.

That night I visit the Krugers to pay my respects. Elga's father, my former supervisor, Mr Wloch, has just died. Elga answers the door.

'I'm so sorry, Elga,' I tell her, 'Your father was a good man. I felt fortunate to have worked for him. How did it happen?' To my surprise, her eyes show no sign of mourning.

'Come in, David. Have some tea with us.'

115

She disappears into the kitchen. Richard motions for me to sit down. He also shows no sign of grief. 'He started coughing last week,' he says. 'By this week . . .' He shrugs.

I sit on the couch, shaking my head. 'I'm sorry.'

Elga returns and hands me a steaming cup. I blow across its surface.

'I can't stay long, I'm on my way to Reinhardt's to see about getting factory jobs for my staff. Would you like me to talk to him on your behalf?'

Richard raises his fist. 'Factory jobs? Support the Nazi war machine? Never!'

'I've heard it isn't safe to be without a work-card.'

He laughs. 'It isn't safe to be a Jew, David. You should join the resistance with us.'

I shake my head, and after a brief and uneasy conversation, we say goodbye.

The next morning Sophie and I make our way toward the little Schultz factory. We trudge through the morning heat along with today's crowd of volunteers. Members of the Jewish militia dot the sidewalks. Their watchful eyes scan the procession.

'We must hurry, little ones,' I hear a young woman tell her three small children as she herds them along. 'We don't want to miss the train or arrive after all the food is gone.'

I don't say anything to Sophie. Both her aunts reported for resettlement yesterday.

In the courtyard of the little Schultz factory, Sophie turns toward the washhouse, and I continue straight on to the administrative offices. Schultz manufactures wool socks and underwear. The main factory occupies the ground floor of two five-storey buildings that stretch from Leszno to Nowolipki. The floors above the factory in both buildings are apartments. The company also has a small warehouse on the Aryan side.

'Good morning,' I say to the middle-aged Jewish woman behind the typewriter. 'I'm David Götzel. My wife works in the washhouse. My good friend Panie Reinhardt is a bookkeeper here. He told me last night I could speak with Panie Schultz about a job.'

'Herr Direktor doesn't speak Polish,' she advises me. *'Sprechen Sie Deutsch?'*

'Ja,' I say, switching to German, 'better than I speak Polish.'

'One moment, please,' she says and enters the inner office.

The sparsely furnished outer office consists of a single desk and two worn chairs for visitors. No rugs cover the wooden floor, and the brown painted walls have no pictures on them. The outside wall has two windows, one of which is boarded over. Through the other, a narrow sunbeam illuminates the dust particles suspended in the stuffy air.

From the inner office, I hear a man's voice exclaim in German, 'Another Jew that speaks German? By all means, show him in.'

Fritz Schultz towers above me. He wears a check coat with a Nazi party pin in the lapel. As I cross the office, he extends his hand. 'What can I do for you, Herr Götzel?'

'Herr Direktor,' I withdraw a sheet of paper from my coat, 'I have here a letter from Herr Eisner, the General Trustee for Jewish Property. Until yesterday I was under his employ. Today, I'm looking for class 'A' positions for myself and each of my staff.'

'And what did you do for Herr Eisner?'

'We assigned apartments, collected rents, prepared reports – things of that nature.'

Schultz nods. 'And how large is your staff?'

'Twelve bookkeepers and secretaries.' I lean across his desk and lower my voice, 'I'm prepared to pay any reasonable amount to procure positions for them.'

He scoffs. 'I need your assistance more than your money.' He sweeps his arm above his paper-strewn desk. 'I have more work than I can handle, and I don't speak Polish. With the help of your staff, I can make more money than you could possibly pay.'

'Then it's settled?'

117

'You'll be my Quartermaster.' He picks a sheet of paper off his desk. 'This morning, I received this notification. All employees must reside within the factory by the end of next week. We've been designated these two buildings.' He points out the window as he hands me the paper. 'You'll be in charge of housing. In addition, you can assist me with hiring, translations, and general administration. How does that sound?' I nod. 'Then it's settled. Frau Goorka, my secretary, will handle the necessary paper-work, new ration-cards and work-cards, all that. Bring your people here this afternoon.'

During the last week of July, my staff and I bury ourselves in our new jobs. Each employee of little Schultz is issued with a new ration-card and a new class 'A' work-card. (Class 'A' work-cards mean production at little Schultz is indispensable to the war effort.) Our 2,000 employees are not to be deported. Every employee family is assigned an apartment above the factory to share with two or three other families. The few remaining original tenants are given factory jobs, and their names are added to our employee list.

Every day, I hear different rumours about the resettlement. One day, 12,000 people are said to have reported to the *Umschlagplatz*, another day only six. Whenever too few volunteer, the Germans institute a blockading *Aktion*. They cordon off a series of apartment buildings and force every inhabitant to report to the court-yard with their papers. Anyone without a work-card is immediately deported. No one knows when or where the next *Aktion* will take place – one day Carmelite Lane, the next Leszno Street. Residents hide. Soldiers and police search the apartments.

I notify everyone at the factory to stay off the streets during *Aktionen*, but they don't always do as I instruct. Occasionally, family members of factory employees are taken away. When that happens, there is nothing I can do about it.

Each night, my staff and I work furiously to coordinate the employees' move into the relative safety of the factory's buildings. I feel our time is running out.

On Saturday morning, 1 August, Sophie follows her new companions as they lug their belongings toward the factory apartment they will all share. Overdressed for the merciless heat and humidity, perspiration bathes her face, soaking each layer of her clothing.

David leads the procession slowly up Leszno Street. On his back he wears a rucksack filled with food. In each hand, he carries an overstuffed suitcase.

Frau Schrieber and Micki follow David. Frau Schrieber carries a suitcase in one hand; with the other, she holds on to Micki, their fingers interwoven. Micki clutches her teddy bear and imitates her father's stride by leaning forward and taking long exaggerated footsteps.

Behind Micki and Frau Schrieber, Nora, one of David's secretaries, carries a small bundle slung over her shoulder. She walks beside her husband, their arms interlaced. He pushes a handcart loaded with clothing and food. On top of the cart, strapped to a sack of flour, sits their baby grandson. He crys relentlessly. The three of them will share one of the apartment's bedrooms. Sophie hopes it won't be next to hers!

Reinhardt, his wife, and her sister walk behind Nora. The Reinhardt's three-year-old son clings to his father's back. They will share the other bedroom. The four children of Reinhardt's missing brother are gone, taken during one of the first *Aktionen*.

At the end of the procession, Sophie walks with Stephanie, Stasiek and Halina. Thanks to David, Stephanie and Stasiek now work in the main factory and Halina works in the warehouse on the Aryan side. The three of them will share the living room.

'Let me carry that rucksack for you, Aunt Sophie,' Stasiek says. 'You look tired.'

'Thank you, Stasiek.' She allows the pack to slip from her shoulders. His eyes glow with helpfulness. 'You've raised a wonderful boy, Stephanie.' Her sister-in-law smiles, but says nothing. Her breathing sounds laboured.

119

At the factory's iron gate, a policeman demands to see their Schultz passes before he allows them to enter. Inside the gate, hundreds of people mill about the courtyard. Stacked in piles along the walls and strewn about the yard are suitcases, trunks, rucksacks, bundles, clothing, blankets, chairs, sewing machines and handcarts.

A bespectacled man with a short grey beard recognizes David and waves a white slip of paper at him. 'Panie Götzel! Panie Götzel! There's been a mistake! This apartment is too small. We must make other arrangements.' As he approaches, a dozen others follow. They all begin to complain at once, and are soon shouting at David and each other.

David yells to Sophie above the din, 'I'll have to meet you in the apartment later!' She nods and leads her family through the crowd to a stairwell on the far side of the courtyard. They go up two flights and arrive inside their new home.

The apartment hasn't been vacant for long. She can smell the remnants of recent cooking. In the kitchen, unwashed dishes fill the sink and spilled food crusts the top of the stove. Down the narrow hallway, the back bedroom contains two double beds and a sideboard. She curls up on the bed nearest the window. The soft mattress feels warm.

She wonders about the bed's previous occupants. To what horrible fate had they succumbed?

A small movement above her head catches her attention. Silky, concentric circles twitch in the corner of the ceiling as a large black spider entombs a future meal.

15 Selections

At six o'clock the following Monday morning, Sophie follows David as he carries Micki down to the courtyard where Halina's work party is preparing to march to the warehouse on the Aryan side. Sophie feels cold – a deep, soul-freezing cold.

As the work detail forms into a column, five deep, David speaks to the group leader and hands him three 20-dollar gold pieces. He then moves Micki and Halina to the centre of the third row. 'Walk with Halina,' he says removing Micki's bright red tam-o'-shanter and kissing her on the top of the head. 'I'll keep your hat with Teddy until later.'

He touches Halina's cheek and smiles. 'Keep her quiet.'

'The child shouldn't be in the morning air without a hat,' Sophie says as David positions her in the second row directly in front of Micki.

'I don't want anything attracting attention to her.' He stands next to Sophie.

After the leader counts everyone, they march out of the courtyard. At the sentry post, the column halts. David squeezes Sophie's hand as the leader approaches the guards. Her heart races as she watches them speak in hushed tones. (If anything goes wrong, she and David agreed to not give up Micki without a fight. David will attack the guards while she tries to escape with Micki.) After several minutes, the German in charge nods, and the work detail leader hands him two gold coins. The workers stand in the increasing heat of the morning sun while the guards check everyone's papers and search for contraband. They search everyone but the Götzels. Then the column marches out of the ghetto.

At the warehouse, Halina reports to her work area while David takes Sophie and Micki to a large, windowless storage room. 'You'll be safe in here. I'll be back later with more food.' He kisses Sophie on the cheek, stoops down, puts Micki's hat back on her head, and hands her Teddy. 'You take good care of Teddy and Mama while I'm gone, OK?'

Empty sacks cover the floor, and chests of grey woollen waste line the walls. Micki removes her hat, dropping it and Teddy as she wanders off in search of adventure. Sophie picks up the tam-o'-shanter and teddy bear. As she brushes them off, wool fibres float into the still air. She looks at David with apprehension.

'Everything is going to be fine, Sophie, you'll see. By tomorrow night, Micki will be safe. And soon, Wanda will find a safe place for you.'

Safe? She wonders if they will ever be safe again. Shivers spread through her.

'Everything will be fine,' he says. 'Don't worry.' She watches him close the door and hears him lock it from the outside.

Evening arrives before the door opens again. David stands in the light. 'You can come out now. Everyone's gone.'

'Papa!' Micki charges toward him.

He scoops her into his arms. 'Have you been a good girl today?'

'It was hot in there, and dark, and I was so bored.'

'Tomorrow you'll meet your new auntie, and she'll take you to the country where you'll get to run and play with other girls.' Sophie hopes he's right.

'Will you be coming with us, Papa?'

'No, just you and Teddy. Mama and I will join you later. But you'll be having so much fun, you'll probably not even notice.' He hugs her again, then looks at Sophie. 'How are you?' She shrugs, feeling exhausted. He flashes her an impish grin. 'Come, *Häschen*, I have a surprise for you.'

With Micki in his arms, he leads her by the hand into a large workroom. On one of the long tables, between two mountains of socks, is a loaf of bread and three small sausages. She smiles at the thought of their first family dinner in months. But her smile soon fades, replaced by an all-consuming sadness. Will they ever be together again?

David sets Micki down and rips off a corner of bread for her. She takes a bite so big she can hardly chew it. David laughs. 'Marysza Zondek will be here first thing in the morning,' he says to Sophie, handing her a small felt pouch that is soft to her touch. So little weight to pay for the life of her child. She opens the pouch. The factory lights reflect off the gold and diamonds. Where did David get them, she wonders, but doesn't ask.

After they eat, David takes Micki into his arms again. 'You be a good girl while you're with Aunt Marysza, OK?' Sophie watches Micki wrap her small arms around David's neck. The overhead lights glint off the tears on his cheeks.

The next morning Sophie wakes with a start. Young girls are chattering while they file in through a door on the far wall. They sit on the benches and busy themselves with the socks and woollen material piled on top of the worktables. Micki raises a sleepy head next to Sophie. They're lying on the mattress they made last night from a pile of soft wool. Sophie didn't expect to fall asleep, but her exhaustion must have won out over her anxiety.

The Jewish girls ignore Sophie and Micki as they go about their work. Some of them sort old socks from new, while others sew seams or trim stitches. They gossip incessantly. Like a kitten, Micki scampers about the floor, laughing and playing in the woollen scraps. Her laughter cuts deep into Sophie's conscience. Will she ever again hear her daughter giggle?

Just before noon, a well-groomed young woman arrives, claiming to be Marysza Zondek. Sophie brushes the wool from

Micki's clothes and hair. Is Mary`sza Zondek this woman's real
name? Is Sophie insane to entrust the life of her only child to a
complete stranger? A complete stranger who requires payment.
She hands her the pouch. The woman looks inside. 'Don't
worry, Panna Götzel. Your daughter will be fine.'

Sophie holds Micki's hand as they walk to the door. 'If you're
a good girl, Auntie Marysza might buy you some sweets or a new
toy for your birthday.' She resents saying it. *She* should be the
one buying her daughter birthday presents – not some stranger.

Micki's eyes light up, and she smiles at the woman.

'She'll be five on the 27th of next month,' Sophie says.

The woman takes Micki's hand. Not wanting to let her go,
Sophie lifts Micki into her arms. When she feels her daughter's
warm soft cheek against her own, she starts to cry.

'Don't worry, Mama,' Micki says, kissing Sophie's tears. 'I'll
be good.' She wriggles loose and takes the woman's hand. 'Bye-
bye, Mama,' she says, waving Teddy.

Through her tears, Sophie watches them go. 'Bye-bye, my little one,' she whispers.

The mid-August sun sets behind me, warming my sweat-
soaked shirt. I stare at the man's dark blue militia uniform and
try not to believe the words he just uttered.

'It's true,' he says. 'They've murdered everyone who's gone
east. I spoke to the man who saw the gas chambers!' The magni-
tude of the accusation has to make it false.

'If this man escaped, why did he return here?'

'To warn us, you fool. Don't you get it? The Nazis are trying
to kill *all* the Jews!'

'How can that be true? Poland alone has over a million Jews.'
And yet, perhaps it is possible. Warsaw's Jews were locked
inside the ghetto before the deportations started.

'Believe what you wish. I'm leaving tonight. And if you have
any sense, you'll get out, too.' With that, the militia man turns
on his heels and walks away.

I lean against the wall of a building and pray that it is not true. The faces of those who resettled flash through my mind: Sophie's aunts, the children of Reinhardt's brother, all the volunteers who marched up Leszno Street – grandparents, parents, children, the unemployed, the starving, the desperate. Each new face adds to my feeling of overwhelming sadness. Can it be? Are they all dead? As the sun sets, I picture the war raging around the world and the earth spinning beneath my feet. I feel dizzy and nauseous and afraid. Especially afraid. Afraid that the stories about the camps are true.

That evening, Sophie's niece, Halina, arrives home from work in tears. Stephanie asks her what happened while everyone else gathers in the living room. 'The Germans came to the warehouse today. They ordered us to the courtyard and took half the women to the *Umschlagplatz*, anyone who looked old or sick. I was so scared.'

'We must be careful,' I tell everyone. 'Keep your work papers with you, look healthy, and stay productive.' I haven't told them about my talk with the militia man.

'What's going on?' Reinhardt asks, holding his son in his arms.

'Who knows for sure?' I tell him. 'But if we continue to prove ourselves essential to the war effort, surely they'll allow us to stay until the war's over.'

'And when will that be?' Stephanie asks.

'Who'd have thought it would last this long?' I look at Frau Schrieber. Her face is white as linen. 'Are you all right?' I touch her shoulder. She's trembling.

'My household chores aren't essential to the war effort.'

'I'll have you assigned to a factory position tomorrow.'

On the morning of 25 August, I sit at my desk and look around our office, a converted workroom alive with activity. My staff has grown to 55 employees. Their desks and chairs are arranged in three long columns. The employees in the far column handle

125

raw material acquisitions and pay bills. The employees in the centre column track shipments and order fulfilment, and the employees in the last column satisfy the Germans' constant demand for reports. I wonder how long we'll be left alone to do our work.

The room falls silent when three SS officers step through the door.

'Who's in charge?' The shortest demands.

I pick up a report and walk toward them. 'I am the factory Quartermaster.'

He looks at my armband. 'Have all your Jews report to the courtyard immediately, and bring your list of class "A" employees.'

'It's here.' I hand it to him. He gives it a cursory glance.

'As I suspected. Too long. Everyone downstairs. *Schnell!*'

In the courtyard, I recognize the uniforms of anti-Stalinist Ukrainian soldiers. (After Germany's invasion, thousands joined with the Nazis.) A hundred of them swarm over the courtyard, bayonets fixed. Some guard the exits. Others pull people out of doorways. 'Everyone outside! Move!' As the employees pour into the courtyard, the soldiers enter the buildings. I hear their hobnailed boots on the wooden stairs as they search the apartments above the factory. Trucks wait in the street outside the courtyard.

The short SS officer orders one of the Ukrainians to fetch a table and chairs. Within minutes the three officers are seated at the end of the courtyard, studying my list. Ukrainian soldiers flank both sides of the long table.

Fritz Schultz arrives and demands to know what is happening.

'Herr Direktor,' the short one states without standing, 'each of your class "A" employees is to line up in front of this table for our review. If we decide they are qualified to retain their class "A" status, we will stamp their work-card, instruct them to pass on the left, and permit them to return to work. If they are not qualified for class "A" status, we will confiscate their

126

work-card, instruct them to pass on the right, and they will board those trucks for immediate transportation to the *Umschlagplatz.'*

'This is an outrage. How am I supposed to manufacture socks for the German Army without all my workers?'

The officer points his fountain pen at Schultz's head. 'Shut up.'

Schultz motions for me to join him by the table. 'Get everyone to line up quickly. Let's get this over.'

I look into the eyes of the SS officers seated at the table. They're about to pass life and death sentences on the 2,000 or so people we struggled so hard to keep safe. Rage begins to churn in my belly, threatening to engulf me. I picture my hands around the throats of these men, squeezing and squeezing until the last of their lives ooze from their useless bodies. I clench my fists, fighting my rage, fighting to stay in control.

Schultz nudges me. I walk over to the gathering crowd and begin organizing them. Once the employees are lined up, the Ukrainians begin removing the children from the courtyard. Shouting erupts as the parents object, but the soldiers ignore them, forcing the crying children through the gate and onto the trucks.

Rather than release their son, the Reinhardts carry the three-year-old out of the courtyard and climb aboard a truck with him. A dozen other parents also accompany their children rather than abandon them to the Ukrainians. I pray that the militia man's story about the gas chambers is not true.

The selection starts. 'Work-card,' one of the taller officers demands. I approach the desk and hand it to him.

'Left,' the shorter one says, motioning with his pen. The taller one stamps my work-card and hands it back. I walk over and stand beside Schultz.

They repeat the procedure with the next two employees, but to the third employee, an elderly woman with grey hair, the short officer snaps, 'Right.' She bursts into tears.

'Excuse me, please,' I say. 'Anna is an essential member of my staff.'

'You wish to join her?' The short officer points his pen at my head.

'*Nein.*'

'Then shut up.'

The procession continues. Left, left, left, right, left, right . . . I clench my teeth and strike my fists against the sides of my legs. Live, live, live, die, live, die . . .

My family approaches the front of the line.

Halina, live. I press my hands to my chest and whisper, 'Thank You.'

Nora, die. No! Her husband steps out of line and joins her on the truck.

Sophie, live. Thank You.

Stasiek, live. Yes.

Frau Schrieber, die. Tears blur my vision. Her factory position didn't help her after all.

Stephanie approaches the table.

'Left,' the officer says.

'Thank you,' I whisper and relax, but Stephanie doesn't move. She looks confused.

'Left!' The short officer commands.

Stephanie looks left, then right. She starts to the left, changes her mind, and goes right.

'No, Stephanie, this way!' I call out to her, 'This way, Stephanie!'

She reaches the far end of the table before realizing her mistake. When she turns around, a Ukrainian soldier lowers his rifle, blocking her return.

'Wait!' I step toward the table. 'There's been a mistake. You said for her to go left. She's supposed to come this way.' I call to the Ukrainian, 'Let her pass!'

The short SS officer narrows his eyes and rises from his chair. 'Did I not tell you to shut up?' He nods to the Ukrainian standing next to me. The soldier backhands me across the bridge of my nose, and the world goes black. When I come round, I am flat on my back looking into an out-of-focus grey sky. My entire face aches, and the taste of blood fills the back of my throat. I hear the procession continue. 'Left, right, right, left, right.' I sit up and look around. Stephanie is nowhere to be seen.

When it's over, of the 2,000 factory employees, only 800 remain.

Sophie labours up the stairs to their apartment with the last three members of her family. She can feel David's arm around her shoulders, steering her body in the right direction. Stasiek is trying to comfort poor Halina who is crying hysterically. Henryk is dead, and now Stephanie is gone. Will Sophie ever see her sister-in-law again? Are Stasiek and Halina now orphans like her? Frau Schrieber is gone, too. Where have they gone? To the *Umschlagplatz*, and then east? Who knows? She wants to cry for them. She feels she should cry for them, but she has no tears left.

When they reach the apartment, Sophie walks to the back bedroom, crawls into bed, and pulls the blankets over her head.

Even over the phone, Wanda can feel the panic in David's voice. 'We have to get Sophie out of here now!'

'I'm doing everything I can, David, but there aren't many people willing to hide adult Jews. I'm trying.'

'Find somewhere, Wanda. Quickly. Please.'

'I will, David. I promise.' She hangs up the phone and covers her face with her hands. Oh, God! Where can she find a place for Sophie to hide?

At the end of September, the SS return to the factory and force everyone down to the courtyard again. To my astonishment, a young woman stands in line with an infant in her arms. How had she managed to hide a baby, and why would she bring it down here now?

129

As the left/right procession begins, one of the Ukrainian soldiers approaches her, his rifle slung over his shoulder, his bayonet pointing skyward.

'The child goes on the truck,' he says, reaching for the baby.

'No!' the mother cries, clutching the infant to her chest.

'The child goes on the truck!' He begins unwrapping her arms. She strikes him across the face. I wince at the sound of the loud, sharp slap.

The Ukrainian backhands her, knocking her and the infant to the ground. 'I said the child goes on the truck. Now!'

'No, please.' She kneels before him, arms tight around her child.

As the soldier steps back, the other soldiers begin laughing at him. He scowls and lowers his rifle from his shoulder, pointing the tip of the bayonet at the woman. 'The child will go on the truck.'

She staggers to her feet and stares him square in the face. Tears stream down her cheeks. Blood flows from her nose. 'No!'

'Yes,' he whispers. Stepping forward, he thrusts his bayonet through the baby's back and into the woman's chest. Her body shudders as her arms fall away from her child. Everyone inside the yard gasps. I watch in shocked disbelief as the woman's head tilts back, her eyes close, and her body collapses to the ground. The soldier raises the impaled baby above his head in triumph. The other soldiers cheer as he carries the tiny lifeless form from the courtyard and pitches it into a truck. My head feels like stone. I watch with detachment as two other soldiers drag the woman out of the courtyard. I don't even flinch when one of them shoots her in the head. They fling her corpse onto the truck.

As if it is happening in a distant fog, I hear, 'Left, right, right, right.'

I look at Sophie. She too appears lost in her own world, deadened by what has happened. When she reaches the front of the line, she moves left as instructed.

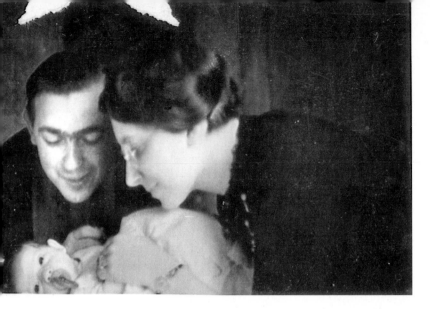

1. David and his first wife, Sophie, with Micki at eight weeks old, in Warsaw 1937.

2. David in Haifa, 1946.

3. David and Micki in Haifa, 1946.

4. The wedding of David and his second wife, Liesel, 1948.

5. David and his mother with Raphael (his son with Leisel), 1950.

6. David, Liesel and Raphael, 1953.

7. David and Raphael, 1955.

8. Micki, David and Micki's daughter, Limor, 1986.

9. Micki, Sophie and Limor, 1990.

10. Sophie, Micki and friend with David, 1991.

11. David, Micki, Limor and Eden, David's first great-grandson, 1993.

12. Micki and
    Sophie, 1994.

13. Sophie and
    Micki, 1994.

14. Tim and David working on the manuscript, San Diego, 1996.

15. David and Liesel, Walnut Creek, California, USA, 2000.

Halina and Stasiek are also among the 400 employees still here at the end.

Two days later, Stasiek and Halina move out of our apartment. 'It's your fault!' Halina tells me, hatred in her eyes. 'Mother's gone, and it's your fault!'

'How can you say that? I did everything I could.'

Stasiek carries their suitcases across the living room. 'You're the only one who could have saved her, Uncle David.' He reaches the front door and adds, 'You didn't.'

'What else could I have done?'

'Don't call him Uncle!' Halina storms past me and out the door. She yells from the hall, 'He's not our uncle anymore. He's nothing! Never mention his name again.'

'Halina, wait. Talk to me.' I try to follow her, but Stasiek stops me.

'It's too late. We'll be fine. You take care of Aunt Sophie. I'll take care of Halina.'

As I watch them descend the stairs, I feel my emotions shutting down. I did everything I could to save Stephanie. If they don't believe me, there isn't anything I can do about that. They are on their own now – two fewer people for me to worry about. The next day, I approve their request to transfer to the branch factory.

In October the selections stop. No one knows why. Sophie and I move through our daily routines with emotional detachment. We eat what food is available. We work in the factory. We sleep whenever we can. But we seldom speak. We've little left to say. Without the threat of deportation, I begin to think the Nazis will leave us in the factory until the end of the war. But Sophie is convinced they are going to kill us.

As the cold rain of autumn yields to the snow of winter, we wait for Wanda to find us two more hiding places on the Aryan side. In the first week of January, she finds one.

16 Escape

Tuesday morning, 13 January 1943. Sophie glances around our factory apartment for the last time, while I search through her few remaining belongings. What else should she take into hiding? Anything to make her life easier, make her feel even a little better.

'Here, *Häschen*, you'll need this.' I hand her a nightgown. She folds it mechanically and jams it into her coat pocket. I tie a scarf under her chin.

'I can't come with you, but Wanda will pick you up at the warehouse.'

She nods. I take her hand and lead her down to the courtyard. I place her in the line with the other warehouse workers and kiss her on the cheek.

'When the war's over, I'll come get you. Until then . . .' My throat tightens around the words, choking them off. Until then, what? I'll pray that you'll be safe? I kiss her again on the cheek, a long kiss on her warm cheek. In the cold still air, my breath joins with hers, forming a small cloud around our heads. I brush a hair away from her eye. It falls back. I tuck it under her scarf.

'Give this to Wanda when she comes.' I put a small pouch in her coat pocket.

Her dark, glassy eyes show no sign of comprehension. I'm losing her. I know it. If only I could help her find a way back to me, protect her, save her, do something, anything other than send her away. But I can't. I cup her face in my hands and say, 'I love you, *Häschen*.' I give the group leader the necessary bribes, and then watch my wife march out of my life. I've done all I can. Her future safety is now in someone else's hands.

For two hours Sophie wanders aimlessly around the warehouse, while the factory girls talk amongst themselves and work with the mountains of grey wool. The warehouse looks exactly as it did when she said goodbye to Micki. The damp musty wool smells the same. The girls' constant chatter sounds the same. Even her sad mood feels the same.

It is five months since she was last here. Five months since she last saw Micki. Will she ever see her daughter again?

'Sophie!' Wanda calls from between two grey peaks. She rushes around a table toward Sophie, dropping the bundle she's carrying. In the two years since Sophie last saw her former housekeeper, Wanda has lost weight. Her blonde hair is now streaked with grey, and there are wrinkles around her blue eyes. But she is still Sophie's best friend. They embrace. 'Is there any news of Micki?'

'I saw her last week. You'd be so proud. She speaks Polish fluently, even says her prayers every night without a fuss. No one will ever suspect she's Jewish.' Wanda retrieves her bundle from the floor and unties the string. 'We can talk more about Micki later. Now we must hurry to catch the next tram. Take off your armband and scarf.' She unwraps the bundle and places a fox-fur shawl around Sophie's shoulders and a large black hat on her head. 'No one expects a Jew to wear fur anymore, and the hat hides your face. We wouldn't want anyone to recognize you.' Wanda hugs her again. 'Let's go.'

Sophie withdraws the pouch and hands it to her. 'David said to give this to you.'

Wanda puts it in her coat pocket. 'Come on. We must hurry.'

When they reach Skolimow-Konstancin, snow crunches under their feet as Sophie follows Wanda through the cold desolate streets. After a few kilometres, Wanda climbs the front steps of a small townhouse and knocks softly on the door.

An elderly woman answers and quietly leads them to the kitchen where her daughter whispers introductions. Anna Maldunek and her mother, Berta, will be risking their lives to hide Sophie. Payment is required in advance. Wanda hands them the pouch.

After they have scrutinized its contents, Anna leads Sophie down the back stairs. In the basement, she knocks on a small door off to one side. From within, the door is unlocked and opened. A short, dark-haired, middle-aged man flashes an embarrassed grin.

'Hello,' Sophie whispers, louder than she intended.

A teenage girl with long dark hair steps around the door. 'SHH!' Sophie says nothing else as she ducks through the doorway.

The little man shakes her hand, whispering, 'My daughter, Margerete.' He places his hand on his chest, 'Dr Piotr Alter.'

Sophie nods and whispers, 'Sophie Götzel.'

The tiny storage room contains a small circular table, an old cupboard, a tattered couch, one cot, and a stove. High on the wall, just below the ceiling, short, thick curtains cover the only window. A musty odour hangs in the stale damp air. Margerete locks the door. Sophie sits on one side of the couch and places her hands in her lap. Wanda didn't follow her down the stairs. They didn't say goodbye. Her two new roommates study her from across the tiny space. She smiles at them and wonders if she'll ever see Wanda again.

Thursday evening, just as the last of the employees file out of the little Schultz factory, the telephone rings. 'David, this is Fräulein Demske.'

'Fräulein Demske? How are you?' It's been so long, I hardly recognize her voice.

'David, listen carefully. You must get out of the Jewish district right away.'

'Why? What's happening?'

'I can't explain now, but if you want to live, get out of there before eight o'clock tomorrow morning.' I hear another sound through the phone. (A door closing?) She lowers her voice and talks faster, 'I have to go. Do whatever you must, but get out of there. Good luck.' I hear a soft click, and the line goes dead.

I stare at the receiver. Fräulein Demske's boyfriend is in the Gestapo. Did she overhear something? Her words ring in my ears. *'Get out of there before eight o'clock tomorrow morning.'* Electricity pulses up my spine. My hands shake as I dial Wanda's number.

'Can you meet me outside the ghetto,' she asks, after I explain what Fräulein Demske said.

'I can leave with the warehouse employees in the morning.'

'I can't go back to the warehouse, it's too dangerous. If you could get to the Hotel Polski, I could pick you up on Dluga Street.'

'I'll be there at seven.' I walk out of the factory for the last time.

In my bedroom, I stash the currency I'll need for bribes in my coat. The rest I squeeze into my money-belt along with the last of my gold coins and diamonds. I'll carry nothing that might draw attention – no extra clothing, no toiletries. I search through my papers for anything important. I have my work-card. Eisner's letter. What else? I see the postcard my father sent three years ago. Along the bottom are the Palestine immigration numbers in strong block letters. If only we had emigrated . . . No time to think about that now. I slip the postcard into my pocket. It's the only thing I have left from my parents.

Throughout the night, I search the apartment. Am I forgetting anything that might save our lives? I can find nothing, can think of nothing, but continue searching anyway.

In the morning, as the work party marches towards the little Schultz warehouse, a light snow begins to fall. From the back of the group, I wait for an opportunity to run. Every day, more

135

and more rumours circulate about Jews being shot on the Aryan side. The snowfall is good. Reduced visibility improves my chances of escaping without being seen.

Three blocks outside the ghetto, the group leader orders everyone to move to the side of the road. A black Mercedes leads a long column of trucks toward us. As the column passes, I see Ukrainian soldiers huddling inside the back of the trucks. The Mercedes turns the corner at the end of the block and leads the trucks toward the ghetto.

I glance around. Except for us, the neighbourhood looks deserted. When the last truck disappears around the corner behind me, I step away from the group and duck between two buildings. I rip off my armband and hurry down the alley. Halfway to the next street, I shove the armband into a pile of dirty snow and cover it.

Minutes later, I'm crunching along Dluga Street and see a black, enclosed carriage waiting in front of the Hotel Polski. As I approach, the door swings open. Wanda motions for me to join her. I climb in. She orders the driver to go. Above the squeaking of the carriage and the clip-clop of the horse's hoofs, I whisper, 'Where are we going?'

'My apartment. There's nowhere else.'

I look out the window to see if anyone is following. If I'm caught with Wanda, or in her apartment, we'll both be shot. By the time we cross the Vistula River, anxiety is making my skin crawl, and I have to fight the urge to jump out of the carriage and run.

Sitting across from David, Wanda shakes with fear. How is she going to get him out of the carriage and into her apartment without the Polish driver getting suspicious, or any of her neighbours asking questions? Thank God, he doesn't look Jewish.

When they arrive at her building, she tells the driver to wait. Despite the cold, she's sweating under her coat. She takes David's hand. 'Careful, darling, the street is slippery.'

She leans her head on his shoulder and hopes anyone watching will think they're lovers. Inside the building she leads him up the two flights of stairs and into her apartment. God must be looking after them for there are no neighbours about.

'You'll have to stay on the couch,' she whispers. 'No one must know you're here.' She motions for him to sit and walks into the tiny kitchen. Several floorboards creak under her weight. Turning around, she whispers, 'That's why you mustn't move around.'

From the icebox, she retrieves a half-empty milk bottle along with the sausage and potatoes she prepared for him last night. After arranging them on a tray with a pitcher of cold water, she carries the tray out to him and sets it on the floor next to the couch. He's removed his shoes, and she sees his little toe poking through a hole in his sock.

'After you drink the milk, use the bottle to relieve yourself.' She goes back to the kitchen and returns with a newspaper, three books, and a bottle of vodka. 'These will help you pass the time.' He looks up at her. Tears glisten in his eyes. She looks around the room. 'I have to go to work. Do you need anything else?'

He shakes his head. She leaves, hoping he'll still be there when she returns.

I listen to Wanda lock the door and walk down the stairs. Her living room is dark and quiet. She's pulled the curtains over the windows. Little light or noise filters through. It's as if I'm back in prison. Actually, prison was better. In prison I could move about in my cell.

The sausage smells good, but the coiled knot in my stomach dissuades me from eating. The vodka is inviting, but I don't want to dull my senses. My head is already heavy from lack of sleep. The milk looks fresh, the water clear, but I don't want to fill my bladder.

The ceiling creaks, and I look up with a start. A neighbour walking to the bathroom? (Something I can't do.) I glance over the first page of the newspaper then try opening it to the second. The loud crinkling startles me. I set it on the floor and allow it to fall open. After reading the paper, I'm relaxed enough to eat the food and drink the milk.

Halfway through one of the books, a sound rumbles into the apartment, the deep, diesel vibrations of an army truck. The knot begins to coil in my stomach again. Will the truck drive past, or will it stop? If it stops, should I run, or is it better to hide? What if the truck stops, but not for me? How will I know? The coil tightens. I wish I hadn't eaten that last sausage. The rumbling grows louder. I raise my knees to my chest, wrap my arms around them. How long does it take for a truck to drive past? I listen. The engine gets louder and louder and louder. I close my eyes. Hold my breath. I wait and wait and wait. The rumbling begins to fade as the truck passes below the window.

I gasp, try to catch my breath. Grief rises in my throat. How long will I have to sit here in fear of every sound? How long before I will see my family? I cover my mouth to stifle my sobs as tears roll down my cheeks. I don't bother to wipe them away.

Wanda returns home well after sunset and quietly closes the door.

The smell of human excrement welcomes her. The only light in the darkened apartment comes from a dim reading lamp next to the couch. She walks softly toward it.

David lies curled up on the couch, sound asleep. The tray sits on the floor holding his dirty dishes. Next to the tray stands the milk and vodka bottles, both filled with urine. Next to the bottles, faeces lie on top of the open newspaper. His unshaven face is relaxed, but she can see the salt tracks his tears left behind on his cheeks.

He has no idea how close he came to dying today. When the Germans stormed the ghetto this morning, they deported everyone they could find. Within hours, they murdered hundreds of Jews in the streets and herded thousands to the *Umschlagplatz*.

She won't tell him about it. He doesn't need to know. She stoops down and folds the newspaper around his stools. The crumpling of the paper wakes him.

'Wanda,' he whispers, a blush spreading across his face, 'I'm sorry. I was afraid I'd make too much noise if I tried to clean up.'

'It's all right.' She disposes of the mess, washes her hands, and sits beside him.

'What happens now,' he asks.

'We have to get you new identification papers and find you somewhere to hide. In the meantime, you stay on the couch.'

His face contorts with pain and fear. 'Will it take long?'

'I don't know.' Wishing to calm him, she strokes his cheek with the back of her hand. His stubble feels rough against her skin.

He presses her hand to his cheek and starts to cry. She pats him on the back.

'You're going to be all right, David. Everything is going to be all right.'

He releases her hand, and she wraps her arms around him. He buries his face in her shoulder. As he sobs, she can feel his warm breath and wet tears on her neck. She closes her eyes. Her body responds to the touch of his hand on the small of her back. It's been years since her body felt the touch of a man. 'There, there, David. Everything is going to be all right.'

His crying slows. She pulls back slightly, turns her head, and kisses him by the ear. 'It's okay,' she whispers. Pulling back a little farther, she kisses his cheek. His crying stops. She kisses his cheek again and whispers, 'Everything is going to be all right. You'll see.' Pulling back a little farther, she kisses him on the corner of the mouth. He turns his head toward her. She presses her lips against his. His arms tighten around her waist.

I awake the next morning disoriented but relaxed. A thick down comforter soothes my bare skin. Looking up at the unfamiliar ceiling, I try to remember where I am. I turn my head to the side. The sight of Wanda's silky blonde hair on the pillow next to me brings everything back.

She's on her side, facing away, the comforter draped across her bare back. I sit up and look for an escape. What have I done? While Sophie and Micki hide from the Nazis, I sleep with our former housekeeper. I can't stay here now – not after this. I slip out of bed. The wooden floor is cold against my bare feet. As I walk quietly out of the room, the floor creaks. I look back at the bed.

Wanda rolls over and opens her eyes. As she reaches up to brush her hair back from her face, the comforter slips down from her shoulder, exposing her tiny bare breasts. She stares unashamed at my naked body and smiles without covering herself.

'Where are you going?' She whispers.

My entire body flushes with embarrassment. 'I'm so sorry, Wanda. This is all wrong. I didn't plan to . . . What I did last night was wrong. Please forgive me.'

She frowns. 'You didn't do anything wrong, David. You needed someone last night. So did I. It doesn't have to happen again.'

I think of Sophie marching out of the ghetto. 'I don't think it should happen again.'

She pulls the comforter up to her neck. 'I love you, David, and I love Sophie, and I love Micki. I don't want any of you hurt. Last night never happened. OK?'

I press the palms of my hands against my temples to ease the pounding in my head. Last night was wonderful. For the first time in years, my life was filled with warmth and love, if only for a brief moment. I don't want to pretend it didn't happen, but it was wrong. 'OK. It never happened.'

Sitting in the afternoon silence, Sophie struggles to adjust to life in the cramped cellar. Dr Alter and Margerete don't say much.

If she could, Sophie would talk to them for hours about anything: their family history, where they came from, what their
home was like . . . Any talk of life before the war would be
welcome. So far, she's learned only that Dr Alter's wife died of
an intestinal obstruction days before the deportations started.
He and Margerete have been living in the cellar for eight
months. When she pressed them for information about their life
before the invasion, Margerete hissed, 'Shut up or we'll all be
killed.'

Sophie knows the danger of making noise. If the neighbours
hear them . . . But she tries not to think about that. She also
knows the danger of silence. The quiet isolation. Listening to
her own breathing. Trying not to think. Wondering when the SS
will shred the door with machine guns and carry her away.
Sitting here with these two, always together, always alone,
always afraid. Afraid to talk, afraid to move, afraid to think.

She looks at Dr Alter, his nose buried in a book as always.
Although kind and considerate, he is a clumsy man. She holds
her breath whenever he moves. Last week, he stumbled into the
table on his way to the cupboard and almost knocked over the
lamp.

She stretches out on the couch and steals a glance at Margerete.
Margerete hates her father, blames him for her mother's death.
She expresses her contempt in cold fixed stares and brief barked
commands that he always obeys. She brushes off any offer of
affection with crossed arms and pursed razor-thin lips.

Sophie rolls onto her back and stares at the dark wooden
beams in the ceiling. As the weeks have gone by, she has learned
the sounds of this house. Anna coughs when coming down the
basement stairs. The cough is soft and comforting – much less
startling than a sudden knock on the door would be. Berta
shuffles her feet as she walks about the house, reminding
Sophie of her own mother when she used to sweep the floors
of their home in Wiesbaden. She misses her mother . . . and her
father . . . and her brother . . . and her sister-in-law. Most of all

she misses David and Micki. But she tries not to think about that.

Sometimes she can smell bread baking, or a pork roast cooking. Nothing right now, though, just the musty cellar. Sometimes she thinks she can hear David's sweet voice on the stairs, or Micki's precious giggle. She closes her eyes. Perhaps she'll nap. She has been sleeping as much as possible lately. Sleep is her refuge from anxiety and loneliness. In her dreams, Micki wears clothes she has knitted for her, and David holds her and Micki in his arms. Surrounded by those strong, protective loving arms, she loses all her worries and fears.

Wanda hasn't visited them for a while now. Perhaps she'll return soon. Perhaps tonight. Every week or so, she arrives late at night, and Sophie is allowed upstairs for brief, hushed visits. Wanda always brings her something, a little extra food, some yarn, a book. Most importantly, she brings news of Micki and David.

Micki is doing well. She now lives under the name of Maria Kurkowska – a good Catholic girl being raised by the good Catholic nuns just outside Warsaw. David is confined to Wanda's couch, but he is alive and well and always sends his love.

A few hours after each visit, the elation subsides and Sophie dissolves into silent tears. Despite the all-consuming sadness that follows, the time between each visit is tortuous. She hungers for any information about her family. But she tries not to think about that.

17 In Hiding

On a bitterly cold evening in March I awake to the familiar
jangle of Wanda's keys in the lock. I sit up and wipe the blur of
sleep from my eyes.

Wanda enters and we begin our evening ritual – the same
ritual we've enacted for the last 40 evenings. She turns on the
radio to muffle any sound and then sits on the couch. I stand,
clean up my mess, and stretch. My legs ache. My back aches.
My pride aches. This night, however, will be different.

Wanda says, 'We've found an abandoned casino outside
Otwock.'

I stop in mid-stretch. 'A place to hide?'

She nods. 'Franc can get you health papers to travel to a
nearby sanitorium. The casino is a few kilometres from there.
We'll leave in a few days.'

I stand next to her. 'How much will the papers cost?'

'Five 20-dollar gold pieces.'

I nod. 'A small price to pay to be free from this couch.'

A week later we arrive at the casino, both drenched from our
trek through the rain. I am wearing a Polish nobleman's outfit:
knee-high black boots, brown breeches, a plaid vest and green
jacket. A short colourful feather extends above the silk band of
my felt hat. Wanda refers to the clothes as my nobilities.

The casino squats before us like an ancient turtle. Bullet holes
riddle its exterior walls. Jagged glass teeth jut from its window-
sills, and bleached boards criss-cross its front door. The building

is flanked by fir trees. Across the street is a soccer field, the goal-posts on each side weathered and bent.

Slogging through the cold rain for an hour has taken its toll. My muscles ache, my nose runs, and my throat burns. I want to curl up and go to sleep. 'How do we get in?'

'Franc said the back door should be open. It leads to the cellar.'

We find the back door unlocked, but it creaks in protest when we pull it open. From the the doorway I can see a flight of steps descending into darkness. I can smell the coal dust, taste it in the back of my throat. Wanda strikes a match and hands me a lantern.

The stairs creak as we descend. I lead with the lantern, bracing myself against the rough wooden rail. At the bottom we find a small room dominated by a huge boiler. The air down here is cold. Off to one side is a smaller room – my new home – probably a supply closet at one time. It is tiny, but at least I can move around. An old bed with worn blankets occupies the far corner. There is a small armoire at the foot of the bed, and a chair beside it. Above the chair is the only window, near the ceiling at ground level.

'You'll have to cover that window,' Wanda says setting her rucksack on the bed.

'How far is the general store?' I ask.

'About two kilometres. This food and water should last you a week or so. When you go for more, remember to take your health papers, dress the part . . .' She looks at me with sad eyes. 'You better get out of those clothes. If you're going to look noble, you'll have to take care of your nobilities.' She gives me a long hug and heads up the stairs. 'I'll bring news when I can.' She blows me a kiss and closes the door.

I'm alone again. This time I not only feel alone, I feel isolated. I listen to the rain drip outside the window. I shiver and change quickly into different clothes. I hang up my costume carefully, leaving the door to the armoire open so it can dry.

After storing the rest of my things, and draping a blanket over the window, I go upstairs to investigate. The building has no electricity or running water. There is a hole in the roof, but it doesn't look as if the rain will leak into my closet downstairs. Dirt and leaves, blown in through the broken windows, cover the wooden floors. I spot four small piles of droppings in the dining area and wonder what type of animal left them. Looking closer, I see the droppings are old. Good. I don't want to share my casino with wildlife.

In the far corner of the building I make a wonderful discovery – a bathroom with an unbroken window. I won't have to risk relieving myself outside where someone might see me, or discover my droppings.

For the next two weeks, I spend hours each day picking dust off my nobleman's costume. It looks perfect. I've also rationed my food and water until they are gone.

When a day without rain arrives, it is time to make my first trip for supplies. I dress quickly and stuff my health papers in my pocket. They say I'm recovering from bronchitis, so I plan to cough loudly if I'm stopped. I strap on my money belt and step outside.

Whenever my father left home he always said a prayer. As I walk, I try to remember his words. I picture him in my mind: his long black beard meticulously groomed; his wide-brimmed black hat trimmed with fur. Whenever he left the house, he always made sure he crossed the threshold with his right foot for good luck, and . . . What did he say? I move my lips and the words come out, 'Now that I begin a new journey, I turn to You in confidence and trust. Protect me from the perils of the way. May I go forth in health and safely reach my destination.' I feel a little better.

The walk should take about half an hour. I keep my head down, my eyes straight, my mind empty. The ground turns from path, to hard-packed dirt, to cobblestone. My heart begins to race and I feel sick. If someone stops me, questions me, becomes suspicious, there is no one to come to my rescue. I am on my own, German accent and all.

As I approach the crossroads my fear grows. The streets look deserted, but an army truck is parked beside the tiny general store. I bundle the collar of my coat against my chin. I can't turn back now. If anyone sees me hesitate . . . I stop at the corner and fake a cough. No one appears, so I move past the truck toward the lone building.

On the wall by the store's entrance there is a large black-and-white poster:

REWARD FOR ESCAPED JEWS
Receive 1 bottle of vodka, 2 kilos of sugar, 1 loaf of bread, and 200 zloty for each Jew turned over to the Gestapo

I imagine strong hands pulling me into the dark mouth of the army truck, while a crowd of peasants points and laughs as they pass around their newly acquired bottle of vodka and divide the sugar, bread and zloty between themselves.

'Nice reward, yes?' says a deep voice behind me.

I fake a cough and turn around. A burly man with scruffy black hair and yellow teeth grins at me. My body shakes with fear. What did he say? I cough again, and again and again, now no longer having to fake it. I nod my head and cover my mouth. My diaphragm goes into spasms. My cough comes harder as if I'm choking on my own wildly beating heart.

He frowns and backs away. I push myself into the store, my heart lurching, my lungs aching. Calm down, I tell myself. I'm Polish. I'm here to buy food. My cough subsides.

I walk quickly around the small dusty room. While I collect a few bottles of water, some potatoes, sausages and bread, I quietly recite my best Polish to myself.

The haggard old woman at the counter doesn't speak except to tell me what I owe. She never looks me in the eyes. I pack my purchases into my rucksack and leave.

Another week passes before I see Wanda. She brings me food and news of Sophie and Micki. My family is doing well in hiding

146

– or as well as can be expected. Wanda's visit is short, far too short. I want her to return soon, but I know the risk she takes with each trip.

Another three weeks pass. I collect enough rain to quench my thirst, and I ration my food vigilantly. Still, I'm forced to buy food twice more, when ravenous hunger overpowers my gnawing fear.

Wanda brings harrowing news on her second visit. When I hear her tap our code (two quick knocks, followed by one, then three) I take the stairs two at a time to let her in. Whisking the rucksack of food from her arms, I hug her tight, and lead her into the cellar, closing the door behind us. She tells me the remaining Jews in the ghetto are fighting the Germans. A sad hopelessness washes over me. I sink onto the bed and picture Richard and Elga Kruger clambering over German tanks, beating on the steel hulls with cobblestones and splintered boards as Nazi gunfire rips through them. I can't get the image out of my mind of my friends' broken bodies lying in a gutter, their blood draining into the sewers.

She then says, 'The Germans have set fire to the ghetto, and they're expanding their search for escaped Jews. In some areas, they're searching house to house. They've also raised the rewards.' She takes a deep breath. 'Travelling is getting more difficult.'

I look at the ceiling. 'I won't see you as often?'

She nods, and I force myself to accept the idea of fewer visits.

'We've come this far.' I stand and walk toward her, extending my arms. She rises to join me, and I hold her tight, not wanting to let go. 'We'll make it.'

A week later, the roar of machine-guns tears me from sleep. I jerk upright on my bed, clutching frayed blankets to my throat. For one frantic second, I can't remember where I am. A tangle of shadows fills the room around me. I smell coal dust and hear wind, then gunfire. I want to scream, but stifle the urge. There is more gunfire.

I wait in the darkness, shivering. There are no sounds from the casino above me, so the gunfire must be outside. The wind carries the sound of laughter, muted, but clearly laughter. I move across the room and step on the chair beneath the small window, balancing myself against the cold damp wall.

Sliding the edge of the blanket aside, I peer through the glass. A light rain mists the grass. Across the street, headlights from two trucks illuminate the soccer field. Six German soldiers order Jews from the back of a truck. They bark their commands and laugh, while the Jews huddle in silence, moving together like frightened children.

I can see what looks like two heaps of clothing or baggage on the ground. There is something odd about those heaps, though. I squint, straining to improve my vision. The edges of the heaps look strange, not smooth like clothing, or squared-off like baggage, but somehow jagged. I rub the glass where my breath has fogged it and stare harder. The rough edges of the two piles suddenly become clear. Arms and legs are tangled together, their joints bent at odd angles, hands and feet protruding. The two heaps are piles of bodies.

The Jews continue to climb down from the truck slowly, mechanically, clinging together in a small haphazard group between the two mounds. Three of the soldiers turn toward them. White light erupts from the muzzles of their guns . . .

I jump away from the window as the gunfire beats against the night. I run to my bed and dive under the blankets. I will never look out of that window again or glance towards the soccer field. I don't want to know what happened to those people across the street. I want only to forget them, forget the soldiers, forget the bodies. Especially the bodies . . .

My stomach heaves, and I force the images from my mind. My muscles twitch with terror, pulse with hatred, as the wind carries more laughter to me. I huddle under my blankets and press my fingers in my ears. I bob my head, slowly, rhythmically.

'Blessed is the Lord our God, Ruler of the universe, the righteous Judge. Blessed is the Lord our God, Ruler of the universe, the righteous Judge . . .'

On the last day in May Wanda arrives, just as the sun sets. She looks distraught. 'It's over,' she says. 'The entire ghetto is in flames.' We wrap ourselves in each other's arms.

After dark, we climb the hill behind the casino and watch the distant glow from the ghetto fires. 'So many lives,' I whisper. 'So many lives . . .'

Sophie sits with Anna and Berta in the kitchen, her hands folded neatly on the table, the taste of fresh bread in her mouth. She feels naked up here in the bright open room, yet grateful to be out of the basement, if only for a while.

'We have good news,' Anna says, patting Sophie's hands. 'We think we may have found a way for you to leave the country.'

Sophie nods without understanding. The window on her right reflects her image against the darkness outside. Anyone out there could see her: an unkempt Jewish woman sitting here. She taps her finger against a half-filled glass of water. The bread melts around her tongue.

They asked only Sophie to come upstairs, not Dr Alter or Margerete. She hardens her heart for bitter news, suspecting that something bad has happened to David or Micki.

'Our neighbours are hiding people, too,' Berta says, her voice light, her eyes beaming. 'The relatives of those Jews found a way for them to emigrate to America.'

'America,' Sophie whispers, wondering when they are going to break the bad news.

'The Swiss Red Cross is providing documentation to the Gestapo stating that American families will take responsibility for them,' Berta explains. 'It's all legal.'

Sophie takes a sip from her water glass. 'What news do you have of my family?'

Anna looks at Berta and back at Sophie. 'We've heard nothing of them. We wanted to talk to you about the Red Cross programme.'

'So, David and Micki are not dead?'

'Heavens no!' Anna laughs. She pushes more bread toward Sophie.

Sophie takes the bread, holds it in her hand, studies it. 'I should talk to Wanda about this.' She tears off a tiny piece. 'She could ask David and . . .'

'There's no time for that,' Anna interrupts. (Since the revolt in the ghetto, they haven't seen Wanda.) 'Who knows how long it will be before Wanda can return. The Red Cross needs the information now.'

Sophie puts the piece of bread in her mouth and squirrels it away in a pocket between her cheek and gum. 'How much do these papers cost?'

'100,000 zloty,' Berta says.

'But the application costs nothing,' Anna adds. 'You just supply them with some information about your family.'

Sophie swallows. 'Does Dr Alter know about this programme?' she asks. She has come to trust him. He is a good, decent man. If he applies for the programme, so will she.

'The doctor has no money for this kind of thing,' Berta tells her.

Sophie watches her fingers wind around themselves. Freedom in America. Her poor David living all alone in a coal cellar. Micki being raised by nuns. Her stomach tightens. David makes the family decisions, not her. 'I don't know if David has that much money,' she says

'Just apply, Sophie,' Anna says. 'Worry about the money later.'

Sophie wants David, now more than ever. What would he do?

'It might be your last chance,' Berta says.

In her fear and confusion, Sophie decides that Berta is probably right. So she gives them the information they need for the application.

Later that night, sitting in the basement chair, knitting a sweater for Micki, Sophie begins to regret her decision. If the information she gave Berta falls into the wrong hands, her family could be found and killed. She listens to Dr Alter sleeping on the bed, to Margerete turning pages of a book, and to her knitting needles clicking together.

Something else is bothering her. Something in the back of her mind, fighting its way forward. It was something Berta said. Of course! The family hiding next door. If Berta and Anna know about Jews next door, don't the neighbours know about her, Dr Alter and Margerete? They must, or they never would have told Berta about the Red Cross programme. And if the neighbours know they're here, why must they stay quiet all the time?

A dark foreboding comes over Sophie. Something isn't right. Will Berta and Anna betray her? That doesn't make sense. If they were going to betray her they could have done so long ago. Maybe the neighbours aren't hiding Jews at all. Maybe they're spreading false hope to people like Berta and Anna, people risking their lives to save others. Maybe they're trying to earn reward money. That must be it.

Sophie can't breathe. Her lungs press against her ribs. She wants to run upstairs, yell for Berta not to take the information. But it's too late now. Berta has already gone. Sophie made a terrible mistake and now it will be she, not the Nazis, or the SS, or the Poles, but she who will cause the death of her family.

She raises her knitting to her face. 'O, David,' she whispers into the unfinished sweater. 'What have I done?' She weeps silently.

I empty my money-belt on to the bed. I ran out of food yesterday and have eaten nothing in 24 hours. My trips to the store, though infrequent, have drained my reserves. I am exceeding my food budget and will have to restrict my eating still further. Hiding is expensive, and this money must last us until the end of the war, whenever that will be.

I decided last night to fetch food today early in the morning. There should be less traffic on the road, and the cold air will allow me to cover my face with my collar without causing suspicion. I dread the trip more each time I make it. Out in the open, naked to the enemy, I walk with a steady pace, head down, collar up. At the store, I purchase my usual supplies from the same elderly cashier.

On my way back to the casino, I hear a truck rumble up the road behind me. I start a coughing fit, pull my collar higher, and turn my back to the truck. As it rolls slowly past, I see Jews packed into the back, unaware of their destination, but probably suspecting their fate. I know their destination is the soccer field. Their suspicions are correct.

Fear creeps up my spine as I walk behind the truck, head down, face buried, coughing hard. What if someone on the truck recognizes me? If they came from the ghetto, they might know me. I wipe my nose with my handkerchief to conceal my face.

The truck moves up the road, stones crunching under its wheels, its occupants silent.

I look up. Blank faces stare back at me, pale, dirty, hopeless. A hollow-eyed woman clutches two emaciated children. A tall frail man raises his arm and points at me. I gasp.

'David Götzel!' He yells. 'Help us, please.' My heart starts beating erratically.

The others join in. 'You can help us, David. Please,' they beg, clawing over each other, reaching out to me with gnarled arms and crooked fingers. 'Don't let them kill us.'

One child, who looks like Micki, squirms from her mother's grasp and tries to jump from the truck to the safety of my arms. I recognize the woman beside her. It's Sophie. She calls to me with dry, cracked lips, 'You said everything was going to be all right, David! You promised everything was going to be all right!' I stifle a scream.

As the truck moves forward towards the killing field, the

152

faces of the victims transform back into unrecognizable blank stares. Their pleas were illusions. I imagined it. My family is not on board. The truck disappears around a curve.

I collapse to my knees, falling forward on my hands, shaking uncontrollably. 'I can't save them,' I tell the ground. My tears drip onto the dewy grass. 'There's nothing I can do.' The bitter wind slaps at my ears, chilling my wet face. I make no attempt to rise. 'I have to concentrate on saving my family. I can't worry about anyone else.'

Later, I walk slowly back to the casino. I don't want to be anywhere near there while the soldiers are across the street.

Back in the cellar, I crawl into my bed without undressing and pull the blankets over my head. Praying helps me to fall asleep, but my dreams torment me. I see myself standing on a hill while thousands of people in the valley below are dying. I am wrapped in warm clothes, a bag of food over my shoulder. I hear them scream, but can do nothing to help. I pray for them, but their screams are too loud for my prayers to be heard.

18 Hotel Polski

Early in the evening of 7 June, Dr Alter sits upright on the floor. 'Did you hear that,' he whispers tilting his head toward the ceiling, his eyes wide.

Fear grips Sophie as she listens closely to her own harsh breathing. Then she hears it. Heavy footsteps. She freezes. Through the wood ceiling, she hears the footsteps clearly, and something else. There are men up there, barking orders.

'Papers,' a voice growls.

Margerete gasps, clutching her hand over her mouth.

Sophie hears terror in Anna's voice, but can't make out the words. Her legs go numb.

'They've found us,' Dr Alter whispers. Sophie looks for a place to hide, but there is none. Even the window is too small to crawl through.

'Hide in the corners. Cover yourselves with blankets,' Dr Alter says, throwing his own blankets at them. He moves frenetically – head swaying, arms flailing.

'Bundle in the corners like rags,' he says. 'I'll do the talking.' Margerete is already concealing herself. Sophie watches with wonder as she disappears into the shadow.

Sophie feels frozen. She can't move. Dr Alter's hands press on her shoulders. He draws a blanket over her. Her legs curl under. The world turns dark.

Heavy footsteps storm down the stairs. Anna's wailing follows.

In the darkness, Sophie says goodbye to her family. The door will surely open, and a bright orange light will flash. She won't hear the gun roar. She'll think only of Micki and her beloved David as the blood drains from her body, and her darkness becomes complete.

There is a pounding. 'Open up. This is the police!' The pounding thunders louder. 'We know who's in here!' More pounding. Sophie tastes her last breath. It smells of sweat and dust and wool. She closes her ears against the madness and tries to hear the sweet sound of Micki's singing, David's soft voice reciting one of his favourite poems. But she can't hear them above the din.

She hears Dr Alter fumble with the lock. The door opens. Men burst in. She bites her tongue, preparing herself for what is about to follow.

'Please, officers,' Dr Alter's voice squeals with terror, 'spare my life.' Margerete gasps. 'She's my only daughter,' he pleads. 'Take me instead.'

The men close in on Sophie. Her blanket is thrown back. A flashlight glares. She wants to scream, but has no voice. Blinking into the circle of light, she sees the steel muzzle of a rifle. 'On your feet, Jew,' orders the man holding the gun.

She finds the strength to climb to her feet, leaning heavily against the wall for support.

The policeman turns to Dr Alter who is being held by two other men, their faces contorted with hatred. 'You are Dr Alter, the former headmaster of a Jewish school in Warsaw.' The colour in Dr Alter's face fades to ash-grey. 'You ran from the Jewish district in August.' The beast moves closer to the doctor, their faces almost touching. 'We know who you are.' He spins toward Margerete, his rifle glinting. 'We know who you all are.' He turns to Sophie. She looks away, can't bear to look in his eyes.

'I can pay you,' Alter moans. 'If you'll let us go. I'll . . .' He bursts into tears.

155

The beast laughs. 'You're a disgrace, old man. Take them away.'

Suddenly, Berta rushes into the cellar, pushes past Anna, and thrusts herself in front of the policeman.

'What's going on here? What are you doing in my home?'

'Collecting refuse,' the monster says, swinging his rifle at her. 'Don't interfere.'

'We will pay you double the reward if you let them go. Please.'

The leader looks at his men. Sophie watches as greed slowly fills their eyes. He leans toward Berta. 'We'll be back tomorrow for the money. If anyone run, everyone dies.' He nods to his men. They follow him out.

Dr Alter sits on the bed. Berta runs to Margerete who is cowering in the corner. Anna walks toward Sophie as the room melts into darkness and Sophie collapses on the floor.

I wake suddenly to a harsh pounding on my door. I fumble in the dark looking for a weapon, something, anything, to arm myself. If they think they're going to take me without a fight . . .

'David,' I hear Wanda's voice. 'Open the door.'

I let her in. 'Why didn't you use our knock?' Her immediate embrace is strong, agitated. 'What's wrong?'

She squeezes my arms, hard. 'The police found Sophie.'

Oh God! I have only one thought. 'What can I do?'

'They want 5,000 zloty to look the other way while she hides somewhere else.'

'And if they don't get the money?'

'They'll turn her over to the Gestapo for the reward.'

'I don't have that much.' I spread the contents of my money-belt on the bed. 3,300 zloty, half a dozen small diamonds, a handful of gold pieces. 'Will that satisfy them?'

She shakes her head. 'They're firm on the price.'

I look at the money and idly finger the diamonds. 'Will they take me instead?'

'If you were to trade yourself, they'd turn you both in.'

I shake the diamonds in my fist like dice. 'There has to be a way to save her.'

'Give me what you have,' she says. 'I'll make up the difference.'

'After all you've done . . .'

'It's the only chance Sophie has.'

'How can I buy her another place to hide? I have nothing left.'

'Franc will find her sanctuary somewhere.' She lays her trembling hand on my chest. 'Let me do this, David. If I don't, Sophie will die.'

I scoop the valuables off the bed and place them in her rucksack. She swings the pack on to her shoulder and runs up the steps. 'I'll be back as soon as I can,' she says, and is gone, leaving me alone in the darkness with my fear that spills forth in great heaving sobs.

Three days pass before she returns to the cellar. It feels like months. Every time the image of what the police might be doing to Sophie tries to force its way into my mind, I resort to prayer or poetry. Today, prayers have been more comforting.

'Sophie is safe,' Wanda tells me. 'She's hiding in Milanowek.'

'Thank you, Wanda.' I lean against the wall, exhausted. 'How did you get her transferred? And don't tell me you spent more of your own money.'

'Franc arranged a place for her. The Underground didn't like the idea of hiding her without up-front money, but certain members owe Franc favours.'

'I'm in their debt.'

We sit on the bed and allow a comfortable silence to envelop us. After a moment, she says, 'I went to the Hotel Polski yesterday. I'd heard the Gestapo was issuing emigration visas.'

'What did you find?'

'A Jewish collaborator, David Guzik, is selling passports to South America.'

'And his price for those passports?'

'Five hundred gold pieces. The buyers are mostly doctors and lawyers who escaped the ghetto with their wealth intact.

They're being classified as foreigners and will be transported to a Red Cross internment camp in Vittel, France.'

I laugh with despair. 'For that price, it's probably legitimate. What difference does it make? Five hundred gold pieces or five, I have no money for food, let alone passports.'

'You might have something better than money.'

'What?'

'Palestine immigration numbers. Do you still have the postcard from your father?' I nod. 'Have you heard of German Templars?'

'The Christian sect that settled near Solomon's Temple during the crusades?'

'That's them. When the war started, many Templars enlisted in the German Army. Apparently, there are 320 Templar family members being held in Palestine, and the Gestapo is looking for 320 Jews to exchange for them. Volunteering for the exchange is free.'

'You think the immigration numbers will help?'

'I think they'll get your names on the exchange list.' She smiles, broad and bright.

I feel Wanda's hope. This exchange could be our only chance. We can't risk trying to hide until the war is over, not without money for bribes and food. I rummage through my rucksack until I find the postcard. 'Show this to the man at the hotel, and ask him if these numbers will get us on the list, but don't give it to him.'

She puts the postcard carefully in her pocket. 'I'll guard it with my life.'

It is three days before I see her again. 'I went to the hotel,' she tells me as she empties her rucksack, 'but not inside. Too many people.' She lays food out on the bed: bread, sausage, pickled herring. My mouth waters.

'Everyone I spoke to verified the legitimacy of the deal. The exchange list is filling fast, and you must be there by the fifth of July or you'll miss the transport to France.'

158

'You're sure it's not a trap?'

'Jews are running both the sale of the South American pass-ports and the registration for the Palestine exchange. The people at the gate knew their names and said they were trustworthy. Those in charge are even sharing in the profits.'

'Good. If they were working for free, it might be a Gestapo trap.' I take the food off the mattress and stash it around the cellar. Storing it separately allows me to eat small portions with-out having to look at what I can't eat. It lasts longer that way.

'The Jews in charge have already procured documents for their own families.'

I pace across the cellar. 'I know Micki will be safe with the nuns until the war is over. But Sophie? Without money, what will the Underground do with her? And the casino?' I shake my head. 'A soldier might wander over here from the soccer field anytime.' I stop pacing, the decision made. 'I'll go to Polski.'

At noon on Sunday, 27 June 1943, my train pulls into the down-town Warsaw station. As I step down on to the concrete platform, I spot Wanda squeezing through the crowd.

She greets me with a kiss that I return, to give the impression that we are man and wife. Arm in arm, we work our way to a carriage outside.

She has brought sausage and vodka, and I eat and drink ravenously on the short trip to the hotel. (I haven't eaten since yesterday.) 'Is there any food available inside Polski?' I ask.

She shrugs. 'Some Jews left the hotel yesterday for food and were shot at by snipers.'

I shake my head in disbelief. 'Is there no end to this insanity? A step to the left and we're safe. A step to the right and we're dead.'

'Just be careful when you enter and leave.'

'I'm not planning to leave. I'm going in there, registering for the exchange, and then waiting for you to bring Sophie and

159

Micki to me.' I see a cloud pass over her face, sadness in her eyes. 'What's wrong?'

'Franc is having difficulty with the Underground. They're making it hard to get Sophie out of hiding, much harder than we expected.'

I fight to control the anger rising in my chest. 'Why should they make it hard? They should be happy to get rid of her to make room for someone who can pay.'

'They're telling Franc to pay, or they won't let her go.'

'She's being held prisoner by the Underground? That's outrageous.' I pound my fist on my leg. 'How do they expect me to pay? I have no money!'

She reaches out to me, her touch soothing. 'Franc is doing all he can. He is hopeful.'

'Hopeful? He's hopeful? First, the German Army tries to bomb us to dust, then the Gestapo wants to ship us east, then the Polish police hunt us like animals, and now the Underground holds my wife for ransom. This doesn't sound hopeful.'

'Franc will know more soon. It will be all right.'

I close my eyes and try hard to believe it. 'I hope you're right.'

The clacking of the wheels slows as we turn onto Dluga Street. I finish the sausage and down the rest of the vodka. It warms my insides, numbing both my anger and my fear. The carriage stops across the street from the hotel. For blocks in both directions, all that's left of the Jewish district is burnt out, hollowed buildings. The smell of smoke hangs in the air as a constant reminder of the lives that have been lost and the sorrow that's been suffered. But dwelling on that won't help my family.

I look across the street at the hotel, a sprawling, four-storey building, the largest still standing on Dluga Street. The street itself is clean, but the once-picturesque square between the street and the hotel is littered with debris. Inside the wrought-iron gates, a solid mass of humanity is crammed into the hotel courtyard. People are everywhere. They stand shoulder to shoulder, sit on the ground and lean against the walls. Well-dressed families. Old couples. Young women with children. The wealthy. The poor. Swarms more stand in a roped-off area just outside the gates, waiting, or pushing to get inside.

'There must be 2,000 people over there,' I say.

'There's probably another 3,000 inside the hotel,' Wanda says.

'I didn't think there were that many Jews left in Warsaw.'

'Many came from surrounding areas.' She hands me a small pouch.

'What's this?' I hear a clink inside the pouch, feel its weight, and know the answer. 'I can't take your money.' I try handing it back to her. 'Give it to Franc for Sophie.'

She refuses. 'You need it more than Sophie right now. If you don't make it . . .'

'I'll make it.' I don't want to hear the rest of that sentence. I tie the pouch to my belt and gather my determination. 'Don't bring Micki or Sophie until I see about the Palestine exchange. Meet me here at eight o'clock tomorrow morning.' She nods. I look up at the surrounding rooftops half expecting to see men with bottles of vodka and rusting rifles.

Seeing no one in the jagged windows, I fling open the carriage door and dash into the street. My knees buckle, but I manage to get my legs under me and push forward, heart racing. For my family's sake, I have to get into that courtyard.

As I run toward the gate, a wall of bodies crams together before me. I'm not going to make it inside. Fearing the sound of gunfire and the spit of bullets at my feet, I dive under the rope and into the legs of the crowd. The concrete rips the skin from my hands and knees. Somebody tumbles onto my back, pressing my chest to the concrete. There are voices all around me, 'Hey! What do you think you're doing? Get out of here!' I roll the person off my back and crawl between the forest of legs. Feet step on my hands, crushing my fingers. Knees shoot painful blows into my ribs and thighs. I've no idea how many people I knock over as I claw through the gates. Still I see no clearing in which to stand. Then there is a small opening and I shoot upright. My shoulder strikes something hard. A sharp pain flares. I wince and drop back to my knees.

'Here,' a man's voice says to me, 'take my hand.'

I see the hand, take it, and am pulled to my feet.

'That was the most unorthodox entrance I've seen yet.'

I brush off my clothes and try to catch my breath. 'I had to get through the gate.'

He laughs. 'I am Yosef Klugerman, and this is my wife, son and daughter.'

'Pleased to meet you. I'm David Götzel. I can't believe how crowded it is.'

'It's worse inside. I've already acquired South American passports for us.' He beams with obvious pride and pats his breast pocket. 'We came out to get some air.'

'Do you know where I can register for the Palestine exchange?'

He frowns. 'Palestine exchange? No, no. You want South American passports. Everyone recognizes their value. With the passports, you're assured safe passage out of the country. The Palestine list is too cheap. There must be something wrong with it.'

'I can't afford South American passports.'

He nods. 'I'm sorry to hear that, my friend. You need to see a man named Engle on the fourth floor.' He points toward the hotel entrance. 'Go through there. To the right is a stairway not as crowded as the others. When you get to the top, turn left.'

I thank him and squeeze my way through the crowd. This is unbelievable. Two hours ago I was alone – a rabbit evading the foxes. Now I'm surrounded by fellow Jews.

At the hotel doors I step into another world. The cavernous lobby is more crowded than the courtyard. Noise echoes off the walls and vaulted ceiling. People cover the floor, stand on couches and chairs, and jam the balconies above. Everywhere, people are shouting, screaming, crying, laughing – an overwhelming crescendo of emotions. To the right is a rising forest of people packed along a railing. They must be standing on the staircase Yosef mentioned. My first goal is to reach that railing.

As I try to move towards the railing, the others inside the lobby resist my getting ahead of them. No one knows how many people will be allowed to leave the country. Those in the courtyard have already secured their emigration. They have no reason to fight newcomers. In here, it's different. Within the great mass of the crowd, smaller separate units press against each other, jostling everyone. As I try to pass, they jab my ribs and kick my shins. The harder I push, the harder they push back.

My hope begins to fade and panic settles in its place. They won't let me through. Determined, I get down on my hands and knees and crawl forward, ignoring the pain from my earlier scrapes. The Palestine list is my family's last hope. I won't be deterred. A fist comes down on my back, knocking the wind out of me, but I manage to keep sight of the railing. Sweat pours into my eyes, blurring my vision. The railing bobs, weaves, appears close, then farther away, taunting me. The salty taste of sweat and blood fills my mouth. My tongue feels thick and swollen. The stale air near the floor reeks of dust and urine.

A few metres further and I climb to my feet at the bottom of the staircase. My lungs ache. My fingers feel broken and useless.

I rub my battered hands together and study the winding staircase. Yosef was right. The stairway across the lobby is far more crowded. The people over there have claimed those stairs for their beds, and no one is moving up or down. Here the people are at least on their feet. They shift and squirm, but make little progress. I won't be able to crawl my way to the top, though. The risk of toppling everyone is too great. I don't want to start a human avalanche that might engulf me. I decide to squeeze up the side. I move around the first row of bodies and press my chest against the wall.

The going is slow, but at least I am not attacked. My thoughts turn to Sophie. We have come this far. We have survived the invasion, prison, the ghetto. I'll get us on the list. But what if the Underground doesn't let her go? Wanda is worried, I can tell. She said 'hopeful', but her eyes didn't show it. What am I to do if Sophie doesn't make it here in time?

Hands claw at my money-pouch. I swipe down, beat them away, and push farther up the stairs. Suddenly I am overcome with grief. I can't leave without my wife. I won't leave without her! Then I hear her voice in my head, 'What about Micki, David? She can't go alone. If I don't make it there in time, you must take our daughter to freedom.'

At the top step, the wall disappears. I'm on a crowded balcony. I pause long enough to look back down the staircase. Desperate eyes filled with exhaustion and frustration stare up at me. On the second floor, people stand in makeshift queues before open doorways. Down the hall, I see the stairway that continues up towards the higher levels.

Fewer people block those stairs. 'Excuse me, please. Pardon me. Excuse me.' I hug the wall, push my way through to the stairs, and climb higher. On the third-floor balcony there are more people, more queues and more open doors. I push my way to the stairs on the other side. One more floor. Now there are fewer people to impede my progress up the final staircase. I don't have to cling to the wall. I just have to show more determination than the rest.

The fourth-floor hallway looks much like the lobby of the hotel, only a tenth its size. Above the crowd, at the far end of the hall, I see a handpainted sign above the only open door. It reads: 'ENGLE – PALESTINE'. Those gathered here are not wealthy doctors or lawyers. These are people with nothing but the hope of getting on a list that everyone else says is worthless. I feel an allegiance with them. I know their pain, their loneliness, their desperation. But my family can't afford me to feel that allegiance. If I take my place at the end of this queue, my wife and daughter might be left standing in the courtyard when the last transport leaves the hotel. And to be left behind will surely mean death.

'Excuse me, please. Pardon me. Excuse me.' I squeeze down the wall and reach the doorway just as a large woman, wrapped in rags, exits the office crying. Her shoulders shake from silent sobs. Once she passes, I peer inside. I smell cigarette smoke, see filing cabinets. There's a lone man sitting at a table. I look back at the queue of people behind me. Their gaunt faces watch me with mild interest. They won't be a problem.

'Next,' the man calls. I step into the room.

Engle is a slim, middle-aged man. He wears a wrinkled brown suit. The cuffs of his shirt are threadbare and his collar is unbuttoned. His tie hangs loose and off-centre. He sits behind a large wooden table stacked with papers. A wisp of smoke drifts up from a metal ashtray overflowing with crushed stubs. Filing cabinets line the wall behind him. There are piles of papers all over the floor. He writes feverishly, looking as though he thinks what he is doing matters. I know offices – I have spent most of my working life inside them. Nothing here looks unusual. There is no hint the Palestine list is a trap; no hint Engle is perpetrating a fraud.

I show him my postcard. 'My name is David Götzel, and I have Palestine immigration numbers for my family.' He finishes what he is writing and sets the paper on the floor behind him.

'Let me see.' He examines the postcard carefully, like a jeweller inspecting a rare gem. I hold my breath as he flips through a stack of papers, scanning each sheet. Halfway down one page, he stops and holds my card beside a column of numbers. 'These numbers are valid. Do you wish your names to be added to the Palestine list?'

'Yes,' I say with a broad grin.

'Many of our fellow Jews are applying for the South American passports. Are you sure you want your names on the Palestine list?'

'I can't afford South American passports.'

He nods. 'You realize there is a minimum fee for transportation.'

165

'This is all I have.' I hand him Wanda's pouch. 'If it's not enough, I could help you with correspondence, or filing papers, or . . .'

'That won't be necessary.' Without inspecting the pouch's contents, he places it in a filing cabinet. He then takes a paper from one of the piles and wets the tip of a pen with his tongue. 'What are the names of your family?' As we complete the forms, I notice my head is lighter, and my wounds no longer hurt.

'You must be in the courtyard with your family on the morning of the fifth, at eight o'clock,' he says. He finishes writing. 'You're lucky, Panie Götzel. Out of the 320 Jews we need for the list, your numbers are 316, 317, and 318.' I thank him and leave.

Heading back down the stairs, I take my time. The weight of the world has been lifted from my shoulders. I try not to think about the possibility of Sophie not making the transport. My thoughts are of reuniting with my family, and finding a place to rest.

19 Waiting

Early the next morning, high grey clouds obscure the sun, and the still heavy air seems to press against me. Wanda arrives at the gates of the courtyard just after eight o'clock.

'We made the Palestine list,' I tell her, reaching through the cool bars to hold her hand.

'I'm so glad,' she says, leaning closer. 'Your face looks like you've been fighting.'

'No fighting, just a lot of crawling and pushing. What about Sophie and Micki?'

'I can bring Micki in a few days. Watch for us here each morning.'

My heart swells. It has been almost a year since I have seen my daughter. 'And Sophie?'

Wanda shakes her head. 'Franc doesn't know anything new.'

I press into the bars. 'The transports arrive in two weeks. She must be here by then!'

'She'll be here,' Wanda says, giving me a parcel of food and two bottles of water through the bars. After we say goodbye, I watch her carriage disappear down Dluga Street.

I spend the next two mornings at the gate, waiting for my daughter to run into my arms. Each afternoon I melt back into the crowd, heartbroken and worried.

Wanda's carriage arrives on the third morning. It rolls up close to the kerb.

My body tingles with anticipation as Wanda steps out, then

Micki. Micki holds Wanda's hand and is wearing a bright blue dress with a flower pattern. She is a head taller than when I saw her last. Grief rises in my throat. Wanda picks Micki up and walks quickly to the entrance as I push myself along the bars. At the gate, Wanda sets her down and points to me. Micki looks up. Her face is thinner, but she looks healthy. She looks wonderful.

I open my arms to her: '*Wie geht's, mein süsses Kind?*' Micki tilts her head, confused.

'She hasn't heard German in almost a year,' Wanda reminds me softly.

My daughter no longer understands her native language? My eyes fill with tears as I force my face into a smile and speak to my only child in Polish – a language I still find awkward, 'Hello, Micki. How are you, my sweet little child?'

A warm smile spreads across her face. 'Papa,' she says and rushes to me.

'Yes, little one, it's me.' I scoop her into my arms. Her body hums with life as she wraps her arms around my neck. Tears spill down my cheeks. 'O, my darling Micki.'

'I missed you, Papa.' She hugs me tighter. 'I missed you so much.'

We hold each other for a long time. When I set her on the ground, I kneel down to her level. 'I missed you too, Micki.' I run my hands through her hair. 'You know, little one, you've grown a lot since I last saw you. You're a beautiful young lady now.'

She spins around and laughs, then stops and straightens her hair. 'Panienka Wanda helped me with my hair. I wanted to look pretty for you.'

'You do, my darling. You do.'

I give her another hug, and then stand up. There are tears on Wanda's cheeks. 'Thank you, Wanda. I owe you so much I can never repay.'

She wipes her eyes. 'It's good to see you two together again.' She tosses me a small bundle wrapped with a towel and tied with string. 'More food.'

I place it in my rucksack. 'Any news of Sophie?'

'Where's Mama?' Micki asks, looking around at all the people in the courtyard.

Wanda looks away. 'They're still demanding payment.'

I clench my teeth, fighting back my anger. 'Is there not something we can do?'

'Franc is doing everything he can.'

'Is Mama here?' Micki asks, still studying the crowd, searching for her.

I calm myself and say, 'Mama will be here soon.' I turn to Wanda. 'I'll talk to Engle and see if there's anything he can do. Sophie's name is on the list. The Underground had better let her join us!' I see Wanda's eyes fill with tears. 'Can you come back on the third?'

She nods. 'I'll do what I can before then.' She climbs into her carriage and is gone.

I lean down and kiss Micki on the cheek. 'Come, my sweet little child, we have to go talk to a man upstairs.' I pick her up and walk into the crowd. With Micki in my arms, I climb the stairs once more. We meet little resistance.

The Palestine list is full. Only South American passports are available now, and there seems to be an endless supply of them, but most new arrivals don't have enough money to buy them, nor do they have anywhere else to go. They stay, hoping for mercy . . . or a miracle.

The stairs, much less crowded now, serve as beds for those who arrived early enough to get inside the hotel, but too late to stake a claim to a hallway. I don't have to hug the wall or fight an angry crowd, just be careful where I place my feet.

As we round the second balcony, I realize Micki doesn't have her teddy bear with her. I pause and ask her, 'What happened to your teddy bear?'

She gazes over the railing, then up at the ceiling. 'What teddy bear?' (What has happened to my daughter? I hold her tighter and continue up the stairs.)

I find Engle bent over a filing cabinet, wrestling with a stack of papers. 'Excuse me Panie Engle. I'm David Götzel, I applied for emigration a few days ago.'

He turns round. 'The man with the visa numbers. What can I do for you, Panie Götzel?'

'My wife has been in hiding for the last few months.' I step into the office, gently bouncing Micki on my hip. 'The Underground refuses to let her go. They're demanding money, but I don't have any to pay them. Could you help me free her?'

'I can't help you with the Underground, Panie Götzel. I would if I could, but they live by their own rules.'

I want to scream: 'But my wife's name is already on the list.'

With some bitterness, Engle says, 'My brother's name was one of the first on the Palestine list, but he died before he even knew it existed.'

'I am sorry to hear about your brother, Panie Engle, but my wife is alive, and you said she must be here by the fifth. Please. Is there not something you could do?'

'I can offer you this. Another transport is scheduled for the 13th. If you wish, I can arrange for your family to take that one.'

Another critical decision, possibly a life-and-death decision, demands an immediate answer. In four days, I can take my daughter to freedom. Or, we can stay at the hotel for another week in the hope of freeing Sophie from the Underground. Will the second transport show up? What if the Gestapo cancels it? And yet, it might be Sophie's only chance . . .

I look at Micki, and then Engle. 'We'll wait for the second transport.'

'I'll make a note of it, and I wish you the best of luck in getting your wife here by then. That will be the last transport, Panie Götzel, there won't be another.'

'I understand. Panie Engle. Thank you.'

While we head back down the stairs, Micki keeps asking me about Sophie. But my mind is whirling, trying to find a way to reunite us, searching for one overlooked option that will get her out of the clutches of the Underground. There are few people in Warsaw who can help me, and only three I trust completely. Two of them are Wanda and Franc. They are already doing all they can. The other is my old smuggling partner, Rolf Schmitz. Rolf just might be able to supply the additional muscle Franc needs to free Sophie.

On the third of July, Wanda returns to the hotel. I had hoped Sophie might be with her, but Wanda comes alone, rushing to the gate in a panic. 'They won't let her go, David,' she says, almost hysterical. 'Franc and I have tried everything, but they're demanding too much money. Even combining what we both have, it's not enough.'

I reach through the gate and hold her shoulders. 'We have more time. I talked to Engle. There's another transport on the 13th. We're now scheduled for that one.'

She shakes her head. 'We can't get enough money, and I don't know what else to do.'

I smile. 'I know someone who can help us.'

Sophie sits in the darkness and listens. For days, treacherous sounds have raged above her head. Heavy boots stamp. Rifle clips snap. Helmets rattle. The tiny cellar where she's hidden this past month stinks. No one has bathed in ages. An elderly man talks nonsense to himself. A woman talks to children she no longer has. A young man, David's age, recites mathematical equations. And another woman sits alone staring at the wall while she rocks back and forth, never speaking a word. The space would be bearable for one clean couple, but five unwashed people create a deadly claustrophobia. Sophie longs for a little room to stretch her arms, a breath of fresh air to clear her lungs.

The people who saved her from the Polish police are tyrants. They toss food into the cellar as if the inhabitants are animals. They snarl commands and deny them light. Still, Sophie thanks them for their kindness. The Nazis will kill her if given the

171

chance. The Gestapo continues to cast out its nets to entrap Jews, and she knows it is only a matter of time before one of those nets closes around her. She hopes to see her family before then.

Wanda visited a few times, but only once was Sophie allowed to see her. Wanda told her about the Hotel Polski and the Palestine list. Sophie doesn't understand why she's still locked in darkness. If David found a way out of Poland, if the transports are scheduled to take them to freedom on the fifth, why hasn't he sent for her?

Days have passed as she waited for Wanda to reappear at the door, hold out her hand, beckon for Sophie to accompany her to the hotel. Now she feels only a sense of hopelessness as the sounds above her rage on relentlessly.

And the one man rambles nonsense, while the other recites equations. And the one woman talks to her dead children, while the other rocks quietly back and forth.

And Sophie will fade away completely if Wanda doesn't return soon . . . very soon.

On the morning of the fifth, I watch a column of trucks roll down Dluga Street. Their tyres crunch over loose cobblestones as a silence falls over the packed courtyard. I hold Micki in my arms and lean against a wall. The Klugerman family stands next to me, bags in hand, expectant looks on their faces. I want to be happy for them, but I can't. All I feel is anger at the Underground for denying me my wife. We should be getting on those trucks.

The column stops in front of the main gate. Stony-faced soldiers climb down and form a line around the hotel. They stand in the street, block the exits, and finger the rifles slung over their shoulders. A crowd gathers across the street to gawk at the spectacle.

One group of soldiers rolls up the canvas flaps of the three trucks immediately outside the gate. Another group positions crude ramps. There are no cries of joy from the crowd in the

172

courtyard. (They've seen trucks like these before. Trucks that carried away their families and friends. How many people have been rolled away to their deaths?) The queues begin to form, and names are called. It's selection time again.

Yosef pulls a small pouch from his pocket and hands it to me. I feel the weight of its coins and the crumple of paper currency. 'I can't take this,' I say.

'We have no use for Polish money in France. Keep it.' He watches the crowd move toward the bottleneck at the gate and follows. 'Good luck, and may Sophie arrive safely.'

'Thank you, Yosef. *Shalom aleichem.*' I slip the pouch in my pocket.

Yosef's wife kisses Micki on one check and me on another. 'See you in Vittel, David Götzel.' She disappears into the crowd which pours out through the gates and onto the trucks.

Those outside the gates find their voice. There is shouting and laughing. Hands are waving in the air. People on one truck begin singing a folk-song. Others join in.

A small crowd of less fortunate people stands just inside the gates. They beg the soldiers to let them through. They wave pouches of money or bottles of vodka at the guards in the hope of being allowed to board.

I see Sophie's face everywhere. I picture the three of us climbing aboard one of the trucks, joining in song with the others. I hold Micki tighter. Our time is running out, and I fear that we will be leaving on the next transport without Sophie. If I'm forced to leave my wife behind, then all my work and all our suffering will have been for nothing. But that is a lie. Micki's future depends on us going, even if we have to go without Sophie.

Sophie is painfully aware of the date. She doesn't know what time it is. She doesn't know what the weather is like outside. She doesn't know when the people upstairs will open the trapdoor and throw down more food. But she knows the date . . . 8 July.

It has been three days since the transport left the Hotel Polski. Wanda said the trucks would leave on the fifth. Providing the Gestapo didn't change their minds about the emigration visas, David and Micki are well on their way to Palestine . . . without her.

The loss tears at her insides, painful, excruciating, like no pain she has ever experienced. She had hoped that Wanda would come, at least to tell her that David and Micki made it on to the transport safely, but there's been no news. Nothing.

Her relationship with the others in this dark space is the same. They keep their pain and loneliness to themselves. She keeps her sorrow and despair to herself. She doesn't wish to know them, better to keep the distance. That way, she'll feel nothing when the Gestapo arrives to murder them all. And she knows that will be the only outcome now. She won't live to see the end of this war. She will never see her husband or daughter again. Despite everything David did to try to save her, she will die at the hands of the Germans, just like her brother, and her father, and her mother.

But not David, and not Micki. She clings to the image of them standing in the back of a truck as it drives down Dluga Street. A truck that carries them away from the Hotel Polski, away from the persecution, away from the hopelessness, away from the death and destruction that is Warsaw. By now, they should be out of Poland on their journey to freedom. That image is all she has left. It will give her the strength she needs to face the imminent gunfire that will put an end to her torment.

The trapdoor opens and Sophie is ordered upstairs. Wanda has arrived for a visit.

'Did David and Micki leave safely?' Sophie asks as soon as they walk into a small poorly lit room and close the door. She wants to know, and yet she doesn't want to know. Her image of them being free might be better than knowing the truth.

'They didn't take the transport,' Wanda says, looking as if she hasn't slept in weeks.

Are David and Micki dead? Sophie's legs give way. If Wanda had not caught her, she would have pitched face first onto the hardwood floor.

'They're OK,' Wanda says, supporting her. 'There's another transport next week. If all goes well, you'll all leave together.'

Sophie tries to blink away the haze that seems to be clouding her mind. She can't collect her thoughts these days. She sees David holding Micki in his arms, running from gunfire. Wanda's face is lost somewhere in the shadows.

'I'm working on getting you out of here,' Wanda says, shaking her. The horrible images dissolve. 'You must be strong. You'll be with your family again. I promise.'

Sophie tries to focus. She doesn't believe what Wanda is saying, feels as if she's trying to comfort her during her time of loss. She doesn't want to be comforted. If her David and Micki are dead, she just wants to be left alone. But what did Wanda say? Sophie whispers, 'Another transport?'

'Yes. So many bought passports, the Gestapo arranged for another transport. You and David and Micki are scheduled to leave on the next one.'

Sophie pulls away from Wanda and stands on her own. She sees David and Micki in the back of a truck again, waving, smiling. This time, she sees herself standing beside them, and she holds on to that thought. Wanda might be trying to convince her that she is going to survive, just to make her last few days here bearable. Even so, she'll play along.

'How will I get there?' she asks.

Wanda glances around the room. 'I can't say anything here. You have to trust me.'

By the afternoon of 12 July, I am in a state of suppressed panic. Micki and I have been surviving on morsels for the past six days, with most of it going to her. Even after eating our scanty meals, Micki still complains she is hungry or thirsty. Finding clean water is getting more difficult, and one question constantly presses on my mind – the one that my daughter asks me, always at my weakest moments: 'Where's Mama?'

I pray that my words, 'She'll be here soon, little one', will become true. But each day there is no news. No Wanda. No Sophie. Nothing. Tomorrow, the last transport will leave the hotel, and my wife is not here. I had thought of venturing out to get her myself, but I don't know where she is. If God chooses that Sophie will not leave Warsaw with us . . . well, there is nothing more I can do. Let His will be done.

I have repeated those phrases over and over during the last few days, trying to lull myself into believing them. 'There is nothing more I can do. Let His will be done.' But they do nothing to soothe my rage against the Underground. They do nothing to comfort my guilt at having failed my wife. And they do nothing to fill this void I feel inside.

But there is nothing more I can do. Let His will be done.

If Sophie doesn't join us, it is His will, not mine. I don't want to leave this place without my wife, but I will if I have to. I will do it for Micki's sake.

20 Last Call

Sophie wakes to a heated argument upstairs. There are loud voices screaming, yelling, commanding. For one brief, terrifying moment, she thinks she's back in her old cellar. The police have arrived. Then she remembers. She escaped from that place. This must be a dream.

She joins her companions huddled together, shivering, heads cocked towards the trapdoor, listening. 'What's happening?' she whispers.

The young man looks at her, fear on his face. 'The Germans have come.'

The room begins to spin. Sophie backs herself against the wall to keep from falling over. Her mind spins with the room. So they have finally found her. This is it. She won't be rescued this time. It will end here, now. She will accept it, for she doesn't have the strength to fight anymore, or cling to childish thoughts of hope and saviours. The only question remaining is, will they kill her here in the dark or carry her off somewhere else.

The trapdoor crashes open. Two of the Underground members run down the stairs.

'That one,' a shadowy figure above yells in heavily accented German. 'That woman, there. She's the one.' The shadow extends its finger and points at Sophie. She cringes against the wall and tries to push herself inside the stone. The two men grab her arms. 'This one?' There is panic in the question.

'I don't have time for your stalling,' the shadow roars. He holds a gun in his hand and wears a long, Gestapo-like coat. 'You know she's the one. Bring her up now or my men will tear this place apart!' His voice is loud, brutal.

They carry her up the stairs, her feet dragging and banging against the steps. She doesn't try to fight, doesn't call out to the others. It would be futile. They have her now. When they reach the top of the stairs, the shadow grabs her by the blouse and pulls her face close to his. 'My men will have fun with you,' he spits.

She feels cold – no fear or sorrow – just cold. A blanket would be nice.

Two soldiers grab her. 'Take her,' the leader orders. 'She's yours.'

They drag her backwards toward the door. She sees the leader level his pistol at one of the Underground men. 'I should kill you now for . . .' But the pounding of their boots against the hardwood floor smothers his words as they drag her backward's through another room. Three men sit on a sofa, held at bay by another soldier levelling a rifle at them.

Sophie wants to sleep, and she would if the soldiers weren't clutching her arms, turning her around, pushing her outside. The crisp night air is cold on her face, but it must be close to morning. The faintest sign of light is just beginning to show in the dark sky. A carriage waits. One of the soldiers opens the door and pushes her into the darkness. The carriage jerks forward, and someone throws a blanket over her shoulders.

'Sophie,' a woman whispers. The voice sounds familiar. 'It's me, Wanda.' *Wanda*? Sophie must have fallen asleep again and is already dreaming.

'You'll be with David and Micki in a few hours.' The woman wraps an arm around her, rocking her gently. 'Everything is going to be all right. You'll see your family soon.'

Sophie doesn't fight the blackness drawing around her. She welcomes it. She welcomes the dream, welcomes the warmth, and welcomes the sleep.

The trucks arrive at the hotel as scheduled, and the soldiers climb down, fanning out around the building as they did before. I feel as if I am watching the scene from the rooftop. Micki stands next to me, her eyes red and sad. She knows we'll be leaving without her mother. She knows she'll never see her mama again.

My pain is immeasurable. Up until now, I've always had one plan or another to get us through. And most have worked. But not this time. I've tried to think of something else, anything else that would bring Sophie to me, but nothing has come. No other plan. No other scheme. No other solution. And all that comes to me now is pain, the pain of my failure to save the woman I love.

I hold on to Yosef's pouch. The few coins and paper currency are useless, but I hold on to them anyway. Even if I had riches to offer, the Underground couldn't get Sophie here in time. Time is moving so fast now. All our sand has just about run out.

I keep my back against the wall and hold Micki's hand. We'll wait until the last possible minute. If we're the last souls to climb aboard the last truck, even if we have to stand on the bumper because there's no more room inside, I'll still wait, wait for the last possible moment and hope for a miracle.

The jolting of the carriage wakes Sophie. Hooves thunder on cobblestone. Wooden wheels clatter. Wherever they're taking her, they're in a hurry. She pulls the blanket tighter around her neck, the warm wool rough against her skin.

'Sophie,' the familiar woman's voice says. 'Wake up if you can.'

Sophie opens her eyes. In the soft, filtered light from the curtained window, she sees Wanda's face, warm and comforting. 'I thought I was dreaming,' she says, still thinking that she's dreaming. At least if Wanda's here, it must be a good dream.

'It's no dream, Sophie. We're on our way to the Hotel Polski. You'll be with David and Micki soon.' Wanda pats her on the knee.

Sophie's mind must be playing another trick on her. 'How . . .
The Germans . . .'

'Those Germans work for Rolf Schmitz, the man in the leather
coat. He and David used to work together. Rolf ordered them
to take you out of that wretched cellar.'

'But the Gestapo . . .' Nothing makes any sense. Is Wanda
working for the Nazis? Did she say the Gestapo works with
David? It's all so jumbled.

'It was a ruse, Sophie. Rolf owed David a favour. This was
his way of repaying it.' Sophie nods, pulling the blanket tighter
around her neck and closing her eyes. Nothing seems real – not
Wanda, the carriage, or this blanket. She likes the idea of being
with David and Micki though, whether that's real or not. It
sounds good, a wonderful dream.

By noon, the crowd inside the courtyard has diminished con-
siderably. Those who tried to board the trucks without passports have been cordoned off in a small area outside the gate.
They wait in fear, their faces drained of colour, their hands
twisting nervously. I wonder if Sophie is cringing in fear somewhere, waiting for someone to come to her and say, 'OK, you've
suffered enough, you may go now.' That's how the people in
the cordoned-off area look – desperate for any chance to survive.
But I know better: they are dead . . . and so is my wife. Tears fill
my eyes as the pain threatens to overwhelm me. Only the soft
touch of Micki's fingers intertwined in mine keeps me going.

People are boarding the last truck now. I've already heard my
name called half a dozen times. Micki tried to go forward during
the first call, but I held her back. 'We must wait a little while
longer,' I told her. She tried to go the third time, but again I held
her back. 'Wait, Micki. Be patient.'

'Götzel,' the man calls again. He stands by the last truck, a
sheet of paper in his hands. Two soldiers stand beside him. All
have faces of stone. 'Last call for Götzel!'

'Papa,' Micki says, 'they're calling us!'

I don't want to move. Every thought, every emotion tells me to wait until I see my wife. But at Micki's urging I begin to move forward. She pulls me through the crowd. She is our strength now. Perhaps she believes Mama will be waiting for us when we reach our destination. Whatever thoughts she has, one thing is clear, she's getting on that truck. It's as if she understands the desperate need for us to leave this place, leave it now. I follow her toward the gates. Towards freedom.

I wave my hand. 'Götzel! Here!' The man with the paper gives me a stern look. I think I hear Sophie behind me, crying for us not to leave her, but I do not turn round to face that vision. (I haven't the strength.) As we approach the gate, I can see into the back of the truck. It's the last truck, the last in the morning's long line of trucks. The faces inside look joyous. I want to be part of them, but I don't feel right. I don't feel whole.

We pass through the gate. I look out into the street and see a black carriage on the other side of Dluga Street. Standing in front of the carriage are Wanda and Sophie, Wanda supporting Sophie's frail form.

I blink and shake my head. I must be imagining it. No! Wanda is there, standing with Sophie. But why isn't she running across the street, helping Sophie on to the truck? I look around and see the soldiers standing with weapons ready. They form an impenetrable barrier between the carriage and us. Only those inside the hotel are going anywhere today. Micki grabs my trouser leg, pulls me forward, straining against my hesitancy. She doesn't see her mother standing across the street.

'My wife,' I call to the man in charge, pointing, 'My wife is there, across the street. They have to let her through!' I can't leave her now.

The soldier looks at his list. 'You have three names here. Give me your papers.'

I hand them to him, my mind racing. I can't take my eyes off Sophie, afraid she'll disappear. Wanda signals me for help. I only have to get Sophie across the street!

181

'Only those present are allowed to board.' The soldier stands resolute. Pleading alone won't help. If anything, it might get us sent to the cordoned-off area. My fingers feel Yosef's pouch in my pocket. I press it into the soldier's hand. 'This is all I have left, sir.' I point toward Sophie. 'That's my wife, right there next to the carriage. Please let her join us.' I point at the paper in his hand. 'That's her name on your list. Please.' I hold Micki's face against my side. 'My daughter needs her mother.' Micki hasn't seen Sophie yet. She wriggles loose, looks into the back of the truck, and studies the ramp, planning her entrance.

The soldier takes the pouch and pours the contents into his hand. He counts the bills and slips the coins into his pocket.

The engine of the truck coughs to life. The people aboard begin to cheer. My chest pounds.

The soldier beckons to one of his comrades, then whispers something in his ear while pressing a few bills into his hand. 'Come with me,' the new soldier says.

I pick Micki up, but the man in charge stops me. 'The girl stays here.' I don't want to leave Micki, but with Sophie only a few metres away . . .

'Please help her on to the truck,' I say to him, and quickly follow the other man through the wall of soldiers and into the crowd.

Wanda pushes Sophie towards me and waves. 'I love you.' Sophie stumbles into my arms. She doesn't seem to know where she is or who I am. I mouth, 'Thank you,' to Wanda, lift Sophie into my arms, and carry her to the truck.

'Let's move,' the man in charge orders.

I put Sophie on the crowded truck, climb aboard, and find Micki among the other passengers. Micki hugs Sophie's legs. Sophie doesn't respond. One of the soldiers clangs the tailgate shut, and the truck begins to roll down Dluga Street away from the hotel. Looking out the back, I see Wanda standing by the carriage, waving goodbye. I kiss my fingertips and wave back.

The afternoon sun bakes the thick cloth that covers the back of the truck. I struggle with the other tightly packed passengers to maintain my footing as we bump against each other. Sophie leans against my chest; Micki stays close by my side. The stench of sweating bodies permeates the stagnant air.

After about half an hour we come to a sudden halt outside a freight station. A passenger train waits for us with bright green trim and red curtains adorning the windows.

We stand in the heat of the truck for two hours, waiting. Up until now, I've seen no disadvantage to being on the much-maligned Palestine list. Everyone has waited in the same queues and boarded the same cramped trucks. But here, those with the expensive passports boarded first and now sit in second-class compartments with upholstered seats. Those on the Palestine list are crowded into the third-class carriages, eight per compartment.

We join two other families on worn wooden benches. A single dirty window looks out on to the platform. No red curtains here, only smears from a child's fingers streaking the yellow glass.

I introduce us to the other occupants, and learn that Mrs Gutkowski and her 12-year-old daughter are travelling to Haifa to join her husband, a lawyer. Mrs Halpern and her two daughters, one seven and the other nine, are also travelling to Haifa to join their family. We smile at each other uncomfortably while the Germans check names against lists, collect signatures attesting to excellent treatment, and hand out food parcels and bottles of water. After one final count, they lock all the compartments from the outside.

It is after six o'clock by the time the train finally pulls away from the station. Cheers rise from the adjoining compartments, and someone bangs on the wall. I hold off my own desire to celebrate until I know which direction the train will travel. When we head west away from the resettlement camps, I relax and offer Sophie some of the sausage in her food parcel. She hasn't touched any of it yet. She shakes her head.

'You must eat something,' I insist.

She says, in a dry voice, 'Save it for Micki, she'll need it more than I.'

'At least have some water.' She nods, takes the bottle we've been sharing, and drinks the last of it.

When we reach the double tracks outside Warsaw, the train picks up speed and races toward the setting sun. Wheat fields blur into a golden sea, and birds circle in the great aquamarine sky. Occasionally a troop train passes us on the opposite track. As darkness fills the compartment, we lean against each other and try to sleep.

Late in the afternoon of the next day, I stare out the window as we pass a small Polish town untouched by the war. It reminds me of Skolimow. Rural life continues. People go about their daily business without a single thought about this train roaring past, where it's going to, where it's come from, or who is inside.

I am still awake later that night when we cross the German border. A ground fog envelopes the train, curling outside the window, frosting the dirty glass. I feel its chill.

As dawn breaks, we reach the outskirts of Berlin. Smoke filters into the sky from recent fires, reminding me of the destruction Germany wreaked upon Warsaw four years ago. I wish I had a bottle of vodka to toast Berlin's downfall. Instead, I drink in the sight of damaged buildings, overturned cars and shredded streets, allowing these images to replace the ones I've been carrying of Warsaw.

Late that afternoon we stop briefly for water in the town of Zelle. On departure, a gentle turn in the tracks takes the train to the right. I glance out the window at the setting sun and realize something is wrong. The sun should be setting in front of the train, not beside it. This window has been facing south for more than two days. I wipe the glass with my sleeve. The sun ripples beyond the mountains, streaking the sky violet and brown, and setting directly in front of me.

I look toward the end of the train, but see only trees and hills, nothing that would indicate . . . Then I see the tracks. There is only one set of rails behind us. I start to panic. We are no longer on the main line. What does it mean? Everyone else in the compartment is napping. No need to wake them. I'm worried enough for us all.

As the sun sinks, the sky turns velvet-black. There are a few stars but no moon. Around midnight, we slow to a halt.

21 Arrival

'Can you see the station?' Mrs Halpern asks. She is frightened. I press my face against the glass and strain to see through the light rain, but in both directions I can see only the shadowy outlines of trees – no station. We have stopped in the middle of a wood. Visions of a dark soccer field on a misty night creep into my mind: helpless Jews standing between two piles of bodies, soldiers . . . rifles . . . I turn my back to the window. 'Perhaps it's on the other side of the train.' Mrs Gutkowski begins to pray, clutching her daughter close to her side.

I hear a scraping outside, the latch on the door lifting. The door swings open, and a blinding flashlight beam cuts through the darkness. A man's voice speaks in German, 'Everyone off the train. Quickly, please.' I can see the uniform behind the beam, the swastika on the armband.

Our journey is over. Despite all my plans, all my work, and all my precautions, our luck has run out. I feel almost relieved. I lift Micki into my arms and grab Sophie's hand. 'I'm sorry, Sophie,' I whisper. 'Please forgive me.'

Surprisingly, I'm not afraid. I must have known this day would come eventually, must have known it all along. The flashlights blur as tears of shame fill my eyes. I squeeze my wife's hand, hug my daughter, and prepare for the end. At least we won't be dragged to the gas chambers to sit in darkness and listen to others die while we wait our turn.

I shake my head and force the images from my mind. I can't

afford to give in to such thoughts. I must be strong, look for a way out. I can't give up.

When Sophie first sees the beams of light flash through the darkness of the compartment, her mind sends her back to the cold cellar, hiding, trembling under the blanket as she waits for the flash of a bright orange light to end her torment.

Then David grips her hand, too tight. She wants to pull away, run, but she can't feel her legs. And the screams are rising. They beat against the walls of her throat, clawing their way up to her mouth. She swallows hard, pushing them back. She follows David's tight grip out into the cold and wet. David whispers something and releases her hand. Now Micki has hold of her. She feels Micki's tiny fingers, soft and warm against her wet skin. She wants to curl up with her daughter and her husband and get back to the thoughts she's been having, the good thoughts, before the running, and the hiding, and the dying. The rain and wind bite at her arms, slap her legs awake.

Beams of light bob across open spaces, flash on trees, scrawl across terrified faces.

Where is David? She and Micki are walking away from him, and he is doing nothing to stop it. The other two women who were on the train with them are helping her, guiding her. Micki holds her hand, soft and warm. When they stop, she bends down and tries to ask Micki what's happening, but Micki looks up with confused eyes and points back to where David and the other men stand, forming a line.

The soldiers begin counting the women. The men stand over there. Why are they so far away? One of the women from the compartment whispers something to her, but she doesn't under-stand. Something about the train being airtight? No, that isn't it.

The SS recount the women. Then they count them again and again.

The wind moans through the trees. Sophie's wet flesh freezes against her bones, but Micki's hand never leaves hers. That soft, warm hand. Small fingers woven into her own. A tiny pulse, faint, but there.

'*Komm*,' one of the soldiers says. She understands that. They move forward. She follows. Women around her speak other words. Words she wishes she didn't understand. 'This is the end . . . gas chambers . . . a trap all along . . .' A woman behind her cries over and over, 'We're lost, we're lost, we're lost . . .'

A truck appears out of the darkness. Where did David go? A man's voice asks them to get in. He *asks* them. No one pushes them, or shoves them, or pitchforks them into the truck. They are polite, and they are not brandishing their guns. Where is David?

Micki lets her hand go. Fear envelopes Sophie as her daughter climbs up the ramp. She doesn't want to be left behind, but she doesn't want to climb into the darkness either. Understanding what the people around her are saying becomes harder. Where is David? Micki, don't go up there. She watches helplessly as her daughter disappears into the truck's black throat. Oh God. Now what should she do? She starts up the ramp and cranes her neck in the rain, squinting through the drizzle. Where is David?

When the SS led Sophie and Micki away, I started to protest, but one of the other men held me back. 'It might be worse if you fight them,' he said. I know he's right.

'They might just want a count of everyone,' someone else says. I watch the women climbing aboard the trucks. My heart sinks. 'I don't think they're going to kill us,' someone whispers. Perhaps he's right. The SS are being too polite. They even help a few women who are too weak to climb up the ramps. Sophie and Micki disappear into the back of one of the trucks. I say a prayer for them as two soldiers carry a limp body off the truck.

Someone behind me mutters, 'Cyanide.'

The drizzle turns to rain. Cold water runs down my cheeks. I lean forward and tug on the collar of my coat. The trucks cough to life and begin to rumble forward.

Ten soldiers stay behind. 'Follow us,' one of them says. The rain gets heavier.

Sophie stumbles as the truck jolts forward. She feels Micki grab her legs.

'Say goodbye to Zygmunt for me,' a woman cries out beside her. 'I've had enough.' Sophie doesn't understand what she means. But turning toward the woman, she sees her drink something. Then the woman falls to the floor and begins choking and jerking about. Micki squeezes Sophie's legs and mumbles, 'Our Father who art in heaven . . .' Rain drums on the tarpaulin over their heads. And after a few minutes, the woman on the floor stops moving.

I keep the slow, steady pace with the rest of the men. The rain slaps at my face, numbs my ears. My face and ears are numb. No one speaks. The sound of the trucks rumbling ahead keeps me moving. The tail lights glow in the dark. They are my beacons. No one asks where we're going. They assume the worst. When the tail lights of the trucks disappear into the distance, I can still hear the rumble of their engines through the rain. That keeps me moving, though my bones ache from the damp chill and my wet clothes cling to my skin.

For an hour or so, we march along the dark, muddy road before leaving the woods. I can no longer hear the comforting rumble of trucks, only the constant splatter of rain and the sloshing of feet. The blackness of the open terrain matches the blackness of the forest we have just left, and that matches the blackness of the soccer field images that now spin through my mind. Two hours later, I see a light, not of the trucks but something bigger.

'Auschwitz,' a man behind me breathes.

Death camp, I think, fighting back terror. I struggle to suppress the hopelessness that now threatens to steal the last of my failing strength. I peer ahead, wiping the rain from my eyes, but it drips back in and I can't make out the source of the light through the blur. As we draw near, I see a wooden sign nailed to a large gate. Lights from beneath the sign illuminate it from the surrounding darkness. The words 'BERGEN-BELSEN' are carved into the wood. Soldiers open the gate, allowing us to enter.

A barbed wire fence, two metres high, extends in both directions, disappearing into the surrounding darkness. Beads of rain cling to its rusty metal spikes. Inside the fence, a tall wooden tower overlooks the enclosure. Through the rain and shadows, I see two men up there, rifles slung casually over their shoulders. The orange tip of a cigarette flares. A plume of blue smoke evaporates into the night sky.

I've never heard the name Bergen-Belsen in any of the horror stories. Perhaps we're the first to arrive here. We march between two rows of single-storey, wooden buildings, dark and empty. I see no sign of my family or the trucks that took them away from me.

The soldiers stop us outside a large barracks. The number 25 is written on a sign mounted on the corner of the building.

'Take any bunk,' the guard says, opening the door.

I want to run, but haven't the strength. Besides, I remember the guards in the tower, smoking casually, as if waiting for an excuse to open fire. I walk into the barracks and steal a bottom mattress near the door. The other men shuffle solemnly behind, filling the three-tiered bunks, one by one. No one speaks. Even after the SS close the door and shut off the lights, sealing us in musty darkness, no one says a word. The only sound is the rain drumming on the wooden roof and the rustle of men trying to make themselves comfortable on spiky straw mattresses.

I lie awake, staring into the darkness, too afraid to shed my wet clothes, listening for the sounds of the trucks that I never hear. Sometime during the night, I drift into an exhausted sleep.

Early the next morning, shouting from outside wakes me. *'Antreten zum Appel! Antreten zum Appel!'**

---

*Outside for roll call!

I open my eyes and stare at the planks of the bunk above me. My head and body feel like lead. Mattresses crackle all around me as people begin to stir.

'*Antreten zum Appel! Antreten zum Appel!*'

'What are they saying?' the man above me asks in Polish.

With a great effort, I swing my legs over the side. My stiff clothes scratch at my flesh.

'*Antreten zum Appel!*'

'What do they want?' The man persists.

'Roll call. Outside,' I whisper. My throat burns like hot sand. My legs ache. And an incessant itching crawls over my flesh, rippling, vanishing, returning.

'*Antreten zum Appel!*'

I move to scratch my side. The itch scurries away, reappearing on my back.

'Bedbugs,' says the man in the next bunk. 'Scratching makes it worse.' It could be lice, but I hope he's right. Bedbugs don't spread typhus.

The door opens. A soldier stands silhouetted against the grey morning light. '*Appel!*' I stagger outside. We form ragged lines, while others pour from adjacent buildings. The people down by the entrance look like women and children. I strain to see better. Could they be the woman and children from our train? I can't see Sophie or Micki, but I'm relieved none the less. If women and children are here, perhaps my family is somewhere among them.

We tighten our rows until we are shoulder to shoulder. The soldiers call out names. For about an hour, I stand on weak shaking legs. The sun rises behind me, roasting my back, intensifying my discomfort. I raise my hand the first two times they call my name. The third time, my hands preoccupied with scratching another elusive itch, I simply yell, '*Ja!*'

I listen to the other groups for the names of Sophie or Micki, but don't hear them. I do hear the men around me scratching, coughing, vomiting. Somewhere in the distance a plane drones.

Finally, one of the soldiers orders us inside and we trudge

191

back to our beds. I collapse on to my bunk, exhausted. I need to hold my wife and daughter. I need to tell them we will make it through this just as we have made it through everything else. I need to believe it.

The soldiers pull three men out of our group and march them off towards a large building. Beyond the building, I can see the tops of four smoke stacks. Crematoria?

Slumped over the edge of my mattress, my head in my hands, I say a prayer for the men to return safely. Will we all be marched off to the crematoria? Will my family billow from the smokestacks and flake the ground like dirty snow? I rub my eyes. Stop it, I tell myself. I can't afford to yield to such thoughts. I can't allow fear to control me.

The droning of another plane catches my attention. German or Allied? Was the plane I heard earlier German or Allied? I can't remember. But from now on, I'll keep track. The sky will be my war monitor. The more Allied planes, the closer we'll be to freedom.

Half an hour later, my earlier prayer is answered when the three men return. The first carries a small black kettle, which he sets carefully on a table by the door. The sweet smell of coffee fills the barracks. What the second man carries makes my mouth water. In one hand he holds a metal bin filled with loaves of black bread, while in his other hand is a bowl of orange marmalade. The third man lugs a grey sack over his shoulder. It clangs when he drops it on the floor. Inside are metal spoons, enamel bowls and tin cups.

The guard hands the bread man a measuring tape. 'Ten centimetres each. One spoon of jam.' Holding up his thumb to the coffee man, he says, 'One cup.' He turns to the rest of us. 'You will receive your meals here in the barracks. These utensils are the only ones you'll be given. Your wives and children will be fed on the same schedule. After you're served, you may go outside with the others.'

Did he say wives and children? Sophie and Micki are here,

safe? Tears fill my eyes as I take a cup, bowl and spoon from the sack. The coffee man ladles the steaming black liquid into my cup. The bread man places the bread and marmalade into my bowl. I eat quickly, my body screaming for nourishment. The food looks and smells far better than it tastes. The coffee is little more than hot bitter water, the bread, crisp salty paper, and the marmalade, thick gritty syrup. I wish I had more.

When I step outside, Sophie and Micki are waiting with the other women and children. I run to them, forcing my stiff legs to cover the distance until they are in my arms. Sophie returns my hug, even manages a smile. Micki frowns. 'There were bugs in my bed, Papa,' she says as I pick her up. 'They kept biting me and biting me.' She scratches at pink spots on her arms.

'Our blankets were covered with bugs,' Sophie says.

'Mine, too.' I point toward the shade of a building. 'Let's sit over there and get the pests out of our clothes. Then we can work on the bedding.'

I show Sophie how to search Micki's seams for bugs and smash them between her thumbnails. They are lice, the same parasites I battled in prison.

After we pick Micki clean, she skips over to where the girls from the train are playing tic-tac-toe in the dirt. We go to work on each other's clothes.

Later that morning, I overhear some men theorizing that this may not be a permanent stay for us but rather a holding camp until the Germans can free up another train. One of those men is Aleksy Solowejczik. Panie Solowejczik stands head and shoulders taller than me. Born and raised in Warsaw, he was an engineer before the war and is quite the intellectual. His German is far better than my Polish. I hope his theory is true. The people who purchased South American passports occupy an area adjacent to ours. They keep to themselves mostly. I don't see Yosef, and I wonder if his family is here.

The guards pace the fence, relaxed, some smoking, some laughing.

At noon, they call us back into our barracks for lunch. We each receive a small bowl of cabbage, turnip and beetroot soup. Nothing else. I sit beside Solowejczik, taking comfort in his presence. The broth tastes watery and bland. Sucking on a rubbery piece of turnip, I fish in my bowl for a piece of meat or potato.

'Anything of substance in here?' I ask him.

'Only broth,' he says.

I look around the barracks. Many of the men are sick, possibly dying. I whisper to Solowejczik, 'Do you think there's a doctor in the camp? If these minimal rations continue for long surely many will get ill.' He shrugs.

Back outside, Sophie and Micki stand with Mrs Halpern and Mrs Gutkowski.

'Micki is still hungry,' Sophie says. 'I gave her some of my soup, but it wasn't enough.' I reprimand myself for not saving any of my soup. That won't happen again. I pull Sophie aside. 'We should start saving food right away. We can hide bread in my pack – whatever we don't give to Micki.'

Later that afternoon, one of the guards tells me that Bergen-Belsen was built as a prisoner-of-war camp, at one time holding 50,000 Russian prisoners. The internal barbed wire fence divides it into sections. Our group occupies the *Sonderlager*, a special section of the camp for transients. We are to be treated with as much dignity as possible. When he says 'transient', my hopes rise. I like the sound of that word. Although the guard is free with his information, he doesn't know if a transport is coming to take us to France. I believe he's telling me the truth. On the train, we signed papers stating how well the Germans were treating us. Is that because we'll be free soon?

Plane engines rumble overhead, and I crane my neck skyward. The setting sun splashes the grey clouds with magenta while the shadows from half a dozen planes jump from cloud to cloud. Except for the engine sounds, the camp is quiet. All the other inmates have stopped talking, and they too strain to look upward.

The planes are too high for me to see if they're Allied or German. They soon disappear from sight, the sound of their engines fading into the sounds of voices around us.

The guards serve soup again for dinner. I take mine outside and give most of it to Micki. Bright floodlights shine down on us, and the guard towers become black windows against the night sky. Children stay close to their parents.

'I don't want to sleep with bugs, Mama,' Micki says. 'Can I sleep with Papa?'

I kneel next to her. 'We have bugs too, little one.'

'Then I don't want to sleep.'

'Don't be afraid of going to sleep, Micki. When you wake up, you can eat breakfast.'

'Will you tell me a story tonight, Mama?'

Sophie lifts Micki and bounces her on her hip. 'What kind of story?'

'A bedtime story. Like the nuns used to tell us.'

'A fairy-tale?' Sophie smiles. Her face is hollow and thin, but I can see her former beauty shining below. 'I might know a fairy-tale or two.'

I tickle Micki until she giggles. 'I'll see you both in the morning.' I kiss them goodnight and head into the barracks with the others. I too look forward to breakfast. The hunger pains have remained a constant, dull ache.

As I lie on my bed, I think about my last meal with Wanda, sitting in the carriage outside the Hotel Polski, eating sausage and drinking vodka. With my eyes closed, I can smell the sweetness of the meat and taste the warmth of the liquor.

I wonder what Wanda is doing now. Sleeping? Certainly not on a mattress swarming with lice, or surrounded by the sounds of the sick and dying. The image of the two of us sharing her bed creeps into my mind. I push it away. I won't allow myself to think of that night ever again, but I do hope she's well. She deserves to be.

22 David's Promise

After roll call the next morning, the men from my barracks are marched to the showers. In the crowded changing room, some of the men start to cry, shivering with fear.

Between the wooden slats in the floor, I see the reflection of the overhead light. Kneeling, I stretch my fingers between the boards and feel cold water. I start to laugh. 'It's a real shower!' Others kneel beside me and begin laughing as well.

Relieved, I stand beneath one of the dirty nozzles with a grin on my face and wait. The water comes on, cold, then warm. I wash away the lice and the fear and the stench.

Breakfast consists of weak coffee, bread and margarine. Instead of sticky marmalade, we receive three small cheese cubes. I put two in my pocket along with one slice of bread. I hide another slice in my pack and then eat my third cheese cube and the last of the bread.

Sophie and Micki have also showered. Sophie looks badly shaken by the experience, but Micki's spirit has stirred. 'I'm clean,' she says, rushing into my arms.

I hug her. 'And you won't be hungry today.' I give her the bread and cheese cubes.

'She had all of my cheese and most of my bread,' Sophie says.

'You must eat too, *Häschen*. You have to stay strong. Micki is relying on you.'

'But she's so thin.'

'If we starve ourselves for her, she'll end up alone.'

196

'Here, Mama.' Micki holds out the bread and a cheese cube. 'I'm not that hungry.' Reluctantly, Sophie takes them.

'Did Mama tell you a story last night, Micki?'

She nods. 'Hansel and Gretel. It was wonderful! And the other girls listened, too. Mama tells great stories. Better than the nuns.'

We spend the rest of the day cleaning our bedding and waiting for our next meal.

We repeat the same activities the next day. We repeat them again the next day, and every day the next week, and every day the next month. Our lives come to revolve around three scant meals separated by hours of delousing. We look forward to our weekly shower to break the monotony. Each day, we wait for news of the transports that never arrive.

On the morning of 21 October, I step outside to a brilliant blue sky. Thick, powdered sugar clouds drift on a dry wind. In their depths, a plane drones, persistent but invisible.

After another gruelling roll call and another inadequate breakfast, I return outside to the sound of names being called. Beside the barracks of the South American passport holders, a long table has been erected. Men and women stand in familiar lines, stepping forward with papers in hand when they hear their names. It reminds me of the factory selections.

A tall man in a dark trench coat paces near the far end of the table. The brass buttons on his shoulders reflect razor blades of sunlight.

'What's happening over there?' I ask a nearby guard. The guards have remained polite, not warm or friendly, but polite. They treat us with a cold respect.

'Adolf Eichmann is rounding up all the Jews with South American passports.'

'Why?' I'm not sure I want to hear the answer.

'They're being transported to a temporary camp near Dresden.'

'Why aren't they taking all of us?'

He shrugs. 'All I know is they're being moved as part of an exchange, but Eichmann doesn't want any authentic Americans or Spaniards.'

'He doesn't want authentic passport holders? Wouldn't they be best to exchange?'

'David!' Sophie calls, her tone harsh and insistent. She doesn't like me talking with the guards, even if it is the only way to get information.

I walk over and tell her about the selections while I give Micki half a slice of black bread and a cheese cube from my breakfast. In my backpack, tucked safely beneath my bunk, I've squirrelled away almost two and a half slices of bread. I turn to Sophie.

'It probably won't be much longer before we'll be on our way, too.'

The next day, trucks arrive to take the selected women and children to the transport station. The men will follow behind on foot. The soldiers help people on board. They even remain polite and patient while everyone says their goodbyes.

I have begun to see the soldiers as defeated children. They flinch when Allied planes rumble overhead. They know they're losing the war, and it appears the Nazis' hatred has become tiresome to these soldiers. Perhaps they thought it would all be over by now and that they could get on with their lives in the New Order.

As the trucks move out, dust clouds spiral in their wake. Cheers rise from those remaining behind. I join in the celebration, yelling congratulations and clapping my hands. Even the men walking behind the trucks manage to raise their hands and cheer back.

The guards move the remaining 350 of us left in the *Sonderlager* into a smaller section of the camp. We men occupy one long barracks building, the women and children the one next to ours. The guards assure us that our conditions of detention will stay the same. I take this to mean we will still receive regular meals and not be subjected to forced labour.

That night, I sleep soundly, despite the lice and the hunger pains gnawing at me. Seeing the others leave the camp has raised my morale. It has raised everyone's morale. Our own passports should be honoured soon . . . very soon.

Three weeks pass with no word as to when those of us on the Palestine list might be leaving for France. More Jews arrive in Bergen-Belsen, but are kept in other areas of the camp, separated from the *Sonderlager* by barbed wire.

Bundled against a cold November wind, I sit in the sun with Sophie and watch a guard force the newest arrivals to work. He orders the emaciated men, women and children to dig into the hardened ground. Some of the holes are to be round and deep, others long and shallow. 'Pile the dirt here,' he commands. I shake my head. I've seen this before. For hours, those poor people will scratch at the earth with small shovels, spoons and sticks. Once the holes are complete, the guard will inspect them, measuring for length and depth. When he's satisfied with the quality of their work, he'll order them to fill the holes back in.

He walks over to another group of new arrivals and orders them to build a new fence the entire length of their enclosure. Later, they will be ordered to take it apart.

I look away. We are so fortunate. The guards have continued to ignore the inmates of the *Sonderlager* (except during roll call, of course). For hours each morning, we still stand in formation while they count, recount and count again. But it's far less painful than the treatment the other inmates have to endure.

Despite the growing number of prisoners inside the camp, the amount of food we receive has remained the same, but I suspect that probably won't last. By rationing our food, I've saved four slices of bread. Not enough to sustain us, but it's a start.

Month after month of inactivity is driving me mad. It's no longer enough to sit with my family. I need something to do. I look over at Sophie. She has become popular in her barracks. Every night at bedtime, she recounts her favourite childhood fairy-tales and fables, or makes up stories of her own, distracting her listeners' attention from the barbed wire, the guards, the lice and the hunger. Some of the women and children who dreaded the nights, now look forward to sunset and another evening of escape into the intricate web of Sophie's fantasies. I wonder if I could do something with the children during the day – perhaps start a small school.

That afternoon, I survey the parents in the *Sonderlager*. They are tired of entertaining the children and are concerned about their lack of education. They like my school idea. Many ask what I will charge. I'm so bored, I would do it for free. So, I tell them I will require no payment, but if they would share a small portion of the additional rations they receive for their children, my family would be grateful.

After breakfast the next morning, I remove two boards from my bunk and prop them against the barracks, facing away from the guard tower. Six children arrive. Using a lump of coal to write on the boards, I teach my new pupils about language basics, arithmetic and the creation of the world according to Genesis. Before lunch, Sophie tells them the story of Little Red Riding Hood while I scrub the boards clean and replace them in my bunk.

The next morning, the same six children show up for school, each with a scrap of food for the teachers. Three students each bring a bite-sized piece of bread, one brings a swallow of milk, and two siblings give us a cube of sugar. I couldn't be happier. By the end of the week, we have eight students, the following week, ten.

In March of 1944 a pregnant women in Sophie's barracks, is taken to the hospital in Zelle to deliver her baby. The following week, she returns with her new baby under a cloud of despair. She has spoken to a man who escaped from the train that left for Dresden.

'Escaped,' Aleksy Solowejczik says to her. 'Why escape? They were on their way to be exchanged.' Solowejczik has taken on the role of elder for those of us left in the camp.

'They were heading east, not west,' she said. 'He paid a guard to tell him the truth.'

'Where did the guard say they were going?'

'Auschwitz.' All hope inside me for any future exchange dies with her words.

Throughout the spring of 1944, the population inside Bergen-Belsen steadily increases. With the increase in prisoners, food rations diminish. Bread servings dwindle to little more than crumbs, and the soup isn't much more than warm water strained through cabbage.

As spring gives way to summer, typhus breaks out, killing scores daily. At roll call every morning, we carry the newly dead out from the barracks so the purple-blotched bodies can be taken to the crematoria that now burn daily. To avoid getting sick, Sophie and I focus on killing lice and keeping clean. Despite the brutally cold water, we wash every day under the outside faucets. The inside showers are now infested with disease and are only used by the terminally ill who might die if doused with cold water.

The end of summer marks the end of our first year here. It also brings an epidemic of diarrhoea. Many prisoners, lacking the strength to walk to the toilets, use their soup bowls for relief. The overpowering stench inside the barracks makes sleep difficult.

In early October, I awake before daybreak drenched in excrement from the man above me. Stumbling into the cold night, I strip off my clothes and wash under the faucet. The freezing water sends my muscles into spasms. Afterwards, I move to a top bunk.

Winter arrives. Every morning, we trudge into the icy air for another roll call. The arctic wind burns my nerves raw while I stand in formation on the frozen ground waiting for the guards to get the count right. Invariably, someone collapses out of formation, or is too stricken with hunger to hear his name called, and the guards repeat the whole process.

Sophie, Micki and I spend our days huddled together to share body warmth.

One morning, I step out of the barracks and see an emaciated man sitting naked in the dirt. His skin is blue from the night cold. He wears a cardboard sign around his neck on which is written, 'I ate a human liver.' I cringe at the thought of this pathetic little man sitting through the freezing night with his dark secret splayed over his heart. And I cringe at the conditions inside this camp that could turn someone into a cannibal.

Toward the end of 1944, the population inside the camp is close to 40,000. When the rations are cut back again, parents can no longer pay for their children's schooling. With less food, my energy fades, and I eventually give up teaching altogether.

Through the extra food the school supplied, I've hoarded an entire loaf of bread. To keep it fresh, I save my bread ration from each meal and eat the oldest pieces. For security, I keep the slices in my pack, and I keep my pack with me at all times. Prisoners now steal from each other constantly, will kill for food. I can trust no one. And the weak, unable to save themselves, quickly become fuel for the crematoria.

In January 1945 parcels arrive from the Swedish Red Cross. The parcels contain chocolates, sugar cubes and dried Swedish bread. The guards give them primarily to the sick, passing on the leftovers randomly. Without those packages, I know many of these people will never live to see the spring.

In March we begin our second spring of imprisonment. New arrivals pour in from camps farther east, swelling the population beyond 60,000. But Bergen-Belsen can't support all the new bodies. Most of the new prisoners are already sick or dying, and being restricted to the camp's food rations kills hundreds every day.

Dark smoke billows from the crematoria as they burn the bodies of those who have lost the will to survive. Trucks circle the interior collecting the dead. But the crematorium can't keep up. Bodies are piled high outside its doors or dumped into mass graves.

I stay close to Sophie and Micki, but feel hopelessness drawing around me like a steel cloak. I fight it daily. To force its weight from my shoulders, I watch the sky. During the day, English fighters streak across it. At night, the drone of Allied bombers lulls me to sleep. The war will end soon. We just need to survive until the Allies arrive to liberate us.

Standing by the barbed wire one morning, I watch a group of SS supervise prisoners piling bodies on to a truck. Micki arrives at my side. Her eyes follow my gaze to the dead. My poor Micki, now seven and a half years old, has grown up surrounded by death.

'Papa,' she says. 'Why do Christians hate Jews?'

I look down at her, hunger pains clouding my thoughts. I don't want my words to sound harsh, but I have little energy to control them. 'We bear testimony that God is one and not three. Since the days of Abraham and Moses and Elijah, man has been taught that God is one, indivisible, alone and unknowable. God placed Jews on earth to serve as that reminder. Many Christians don't like to be reminded of the error in their beliefs.'

She keeps her gaze fixed on the army truck as she twirls a small stick with her fingers. 'What happens to us when we die?' she asks, not looking up. I don't want to have this conversation with my daughter, not here, not now. But I'd like her to know how I see things. So I try to explain: 'After death, your body becomes food for the earth, but the meaning of your life goes on. From the day you are born, you add meaning to your life by your deeds. It's not your achievements or fame that give your life meaning, but the deeds you do. Sharing your successes and your tragedies with those around you, those you love, is what remains alive and remembered after your body is gone. If a person has no family, no children, no one to share their life with; if they are just by themselves and don't perform any good deeds for others, then when they die, it's as if they never lived.'

As the words escape my lips, a deep sense of release spreads through me. I've kept so much bottled up, things I haven't expressed for so long. Micki wraps her arms around my legs and looks toward Sophie who is sitting alone by the barracks, staring into the distance.

'Even nuns who see Jesus as their bridegroom and follow in the footsteps of His words, have no value in life if they do nothing for humanity. If they live only for their own redemption, then they have lived a selfish life. But if a nun becomes a nurse and heals the sick, then she becomes a valuable part of humanity and will be remembered.'

I stoop down and sit crosslegged on the cool dirt. Micki makes herself comfortable in my lap, still twirling the stick through her fingers. 'What happens to our souls when we die? The nuns talked a lot about our souls.'

'Well, when you die, it's your body that dies. Your soul lives on through those who remember you, your family, your children, and those you help during your life. Your soul can only live on in the minds and hearts of those you leave behind.'

'So your soul will be in me when you die?'

I nod. 'My soul will live strong within you because I love you so much.'

'And Mama's soul will live in me, too?'

'Mama's soul and the souls of all the people who have done good things for you. And your heart is so big it will be able to hold every one.'

'What about heaven?'

My mind is open and relaxed. I haven't spoken of my beliefs for years, partly out of a fear that they had changed, not sure what I believe anymore. Hasn't so much of what I thought was true turned false under the harsh glare of death and destruction?

'My parents, your grandparents, believe in heaven. They believe it's the place where the righteous sit at a long table with God. Those who don't sit at the table end up in hell. Hell isn't fiery torture and pain, though. It's hell simply because it isn't paradise. But I don't believe in heaven or hell. The Torah says nothing about life after death. That's a concept from the Christians' New Testament.'

Micki yawns. 'I'm going to go sit with Mama.' She kisses my cheek, and runs across the yard. I brush the dirt off my pants and stare at the trucks moving down the rows of barracks, loading bodies, clearing away the dead. I want to speak to God. It's been a long time since I spoke with my Creator. I look toward the clouds.

'My name is David, son of Joseph Raphael. I have nothing to repent, nothing to return to. I have done all I can to perform good deeds for others.' I feel the conversation turning in my mind. The lives of my family depend on Him. 'I'd like to make a deal with You. If You will help my family survive this difficult time, I promise to buy a Torah, no matter the cost, and dedicate it to You and follow its covenants for the rest of my life.'

The roar of engines rumbles above, and I turn my head toward the sound. Allied bombers darken the sky, and I gather strength from the sight. Whatever happens from this point forward, I know we will survive. God is on our side. The Allies will win . . . but when?

I look back at Micki sitting on Sophie's lap, Sophie mechanically delousing her. My family is rail thin, not much more than skin stretched over bone. With their dark eyes deeply recessed into their sockets, they look much like the bodies piled around the camp. I can't allow them to lose any more weight. We'll have to start eating our savings. Even with that, I won't be able to keep them alive much longer.

I look back up to my Creator. 'Please, let it end soon.'

23 Liberation

On Friday evening, 6 April 1945, the guards assemble the remaining residents of the *Sonderlager* outside our barracks. The comforting rumble of Allied bombers rolls across the dark sky as I join Sophie and Micki.

I ask Sophie how her dinner was. She shrugs. I divide half a slice of hoarded bread between us. I can almost see through Sophie's skin, and a dull sheen covers her eyes. Starvation is draining her; hopelessness consuming her. I've watched it happen, helpless to stop it. I look about as deathly. When I bathe, I can see my ribs covered only by a thin veil of flesh. Just getting dressed drains all my energy. It is the same for everyone. Carrying the kettle from the kitchen is now a three-man job.

Although my body is wasting away, my heart still beats with faith, and the strength of that faith keeps my mind alive. I have tried to transfer that inner strength to Sophie. I have prayed with her and pointed out Allied aircraft. But she remains shut off from me, drifting further away every day. Telling stories to the children had helped her to rally. But many of those children are gone now, and their parents no longer wish to hear fairy-tales.

'Bring your belongings to morning roll-call,' a guard says when we are gathered together. 'You are being evacuated to Theresienstadt in Czechoslovakia. Immediately after roll-call tomorrow, you will walk to the train. Those too weak or sick are to stay here. We will have no patience for anyone falling behind.' He leaves us standing here in the dark.

Everyone remains silent. I put my arm around Sophie and wonder, is this good news, or bad? Everyone is weak or sick, are they giving us a choice whether to go or stay?

A long, silent moment passes before people begin moving around, whispering. I would like to hear what the camp elder thinks. I look around for Aleksy Solowejczik, but can't find him. Many in the *Sonderlager* are joyous, hugging each other. Others look as I feel, torn between thought and feeling. I know we must leave. The food rations, what's left of them, could stop at any time. With Sophie near death, what choice do we have? But what if the evacuation is another Nazi trick, another route to Auschwitz?

'What are we going to do,' Sophie asks. I look back on the decisions that helped us get this far. For six years, I've chosen courses of action over passivity, never passing up an opportunity to do something. That way of thinking has kept us alive. I will do the same now. I wrap my arms around Sophie and Micki. 'We'll leave tomorrow and see what awaits us in Theresienstadt.'

That night, the barracks are alive with voices: 'Where are they *really* taking the fools who go?' . . . 'They're going to kill anyone who stays!'

I sit with Aleksy Solowejczik. 'What do you think of all this?' I ask him.

'If they wanted to kill us, they could have done so long ago. No one has the strength to fight.' He glances out the window at the sound of another plane. 'The Allies must be close, or the Germans wouldn't be evacuating the camp. The question is: if you stay behind, will you be liberated or will they kill everyone before the Allies arrive?'

The next morning greets us with a frigid wind blowing across fields of ice. I wrap the tattered remnants of our blankets around Sophie and Micki.

Roll-call goes smoothly, many having found strength in knowing that they are leaving. I feel my own strength blossom as we, and the other 200 surviving members of the *Sonderlager*, join some 2,000 other evacuees walking and stumbling towards the gate. We have survived this camp. We have survived everything Hitler has thrown at us.

We march past scattered corpses awaiting the crematoria trucks. The people staying behind wave goodbye with twig-thin arms, and wish us good luck.

Sophie walks slowly beside me, her face down. Micki walks ahead, her step almost light – a splash of life amongst the dead and dying. A loose column funnels out of the front gates and on to the gravel road that brought us into the camp almost two years ago. Stones crunch under our feet as we walk. The temperature rises quickly with the morning sun.

Within an hour, the slow-moving column stretches a kilometre alongside the road. I see several charred craters where bombs have left their mark on the barren landscape. We stop every hundred metres or so to rest and wipe the sweat from our faces. A man in front of us shares a slice of bread with Micki, and the SS comes by with a canteen of warm water. Sophie grows weaker as our journey continues. We fall farther behind. I help her as best I can, supporting some of her weight, but I am losing strength too.

We enter a small wood and the shelter of pine trees offers cool comfort. It's been a long time since I smelled trees. We march past a small cottage tucked off to the side of the road. Bright green and blue curtains adorn the windows. A bicycle leans against the gate. I hope that someday we will live in a normal house again and have a normal life.

The three of us are among the last to arrive at the railroad siding – the same one where we were originally dropped off. A passenger train waits.

'We'll rest soon,' I tell Sophie. She leans against me, breathing heavily.

As people cram into the compartments of the train, none of the 50 or so guards who escorted us give any orders. I watch as one man pushes a woman off the steps. He screams like a wild animal and leaps into the compartment. Fear begins to rise in my chest. There aren't enough compartments on the train. We must hurry or we'll be left behind. And then what? Will they drag us back to Bergen-Belsen or slaughter us here?

'Micki,' I say, fighting off panic. 'Help Mama the rest of the way. I'll find us space.'

I race the length of the train, searching each compartment for room. People on board scream at me when I climb their steps. Those outside brush hard against me, bone to bone, growling, muttering curses. The guards, indifferent to the chaos, keep their eyes focused on the surrounding trees, making sure no one tries to escape.

I look back at Sophie and Micki, now waiting beside the train. Almost everyone else is on board. I feel the same panic that I felt in the Hotel Polski. Not one friendly face. Not one offer of assistance. At the rear of the train, I find a compartment with six women inside. It's crowded, but there's room for three more.

I turn and call, 'Micki!' She looks over at me. 'Bring Mama here!'

One of the women shrieks, 'There's no room in here for you!'

I hear Micki behind me, urging Sophie forward.

Another woman begins to wail, 'We won't be able to breathe!'

'There's plenty of room.' I'm getting into this compartment with my family even if I have to stretch myself across the laps of these women. I help Sophie up the steps.

Whether because of Sophie's weakened state or Micki's angelic face I don't know, but the women move enough to allow Sophie and Micki space on the wooden bench. I take a spot on the floor, grateful to be off my feet. A tense silence fills the compartment. I decide not to make introductions – better we all remain nameless.

Minutes drag into hours. The train doesn't move. Sophie rests her head against Micki and drifts off to sleep. A soldier comes by and says, 'The engine hasn't arrived yet. If you need to relieve yourselves, use the woods.' He leaves us to our silence.

By dusk, everyone in the compartment is asleep. I watch Sophie, imagining her younger and healthier body running down the streets of Paris in spring. Micki's tiny chest rises and falls rhythmically. The other women's knuckles pale as they grip their worn bags. I pray continuously. Sometime during the night, I manage to fall into a dreamless sleep.

I wake at dawn to Micki patting me gently on the shoulder. 'Here, Papa,' she says, handing me a piece of dark bread. I'm not sure where I am. When I move, my legs come alive with hot needles of pain, and my back aches dreadfully from sleeping on the floor.

'Where did you get the bread?' I take a large bite and begin rolling my shoulders and stretching my joints. Like old metal hinges, my bones scrape against each other. One of the women says, 'A guard came by and passed out water and a loaf of bread to each compartment.' She frowns. 'Your wife is very sick.'

I look at Sophie. She is still asleep, her flesh deathly pale. Her breath comes and goes in shallow, irregular hitches and there is a greasy sheen of sweat on her forehead. I move toward her, letting Micki do her best to support me. 'Mama woke up and ate a little bread. Then she just went back to sleep.'

I wipe the sweat from Sophie's forehead. She has a fever. I tear off a strip of my shirt, pour water on it, and dab her face. 'Did the guard say when we'd be leaving?'

'Perhaps this afternoon,' she says, 'he wasn't sure.' Micki sits on the floor and wraps her fingers around her mother's thin hand.

I fight back the tears that threaten to drown me. I won't lose Sophie now, not after all we have endured. I listen to her breath, like the sound of a dying engine, slowing, halting, slowing. I look for comfort in the faces of the women, but they look away.

I take another bite from my bread, and then clear my throat. 'Micki, do you remember the stories Mama used to tell?'

She nods, her eyes wide, innocent. 'Fairy-tales.'

210

'I bet Mama would love to hear one of them now.' Micki looks at Sophie, and her bright eyes cloud.

'I'm sure the nice ladies would like to hear a good story, too.' I run my hand through her thinning hair. 'I know I would.'

'I'd like to hear a fairy-tale,' the woman next to Sophie says.

I look at Micki, 'Do you have a favourite? One that Mama would like?'

'I like the one about Hansel and Gretel.'

'That will be fine.'

I hold Sophie's cool hand in mine and listen to Micki's sweet voice recite the tale. She makes up the parts she can't remember, and that makes me smile. Halfway through the story, Sophie's hand begins to warm, and her breathing improves, just a little. It sounds steadier, not quite as harsh or broken. Micki's voice soothes us all, and no one objects when she finishes her tale and begins another.

The engine arrives at dawn the next morning, and the train rumbles into motion. Sophie stirs at the sudden rocking, but doesn't wake. Micki looks out the window. The tracks carry us south, then east toward Zelle. I stand by the window, shifting my weight from side to side. We're going deeper into Germany, away from the American and British troops. Throughout the day, the brakes scream, bringing us to a halt. We then sit motionless on the tracks, sometimes an hour or more, with no explanation from the guards.

That night, I see bombs explode in the distance, then draw closer. The train screeches to a halt. Sophie falls off the bench and screams. Micki follows with a high-pitched wail. Several of the women begin crying.

'Everyone off the train!' The guards outside scream, 'Now! Everyone off!'

There's a deafening roar of aircraft, as if they are on top of us. A bomb explodes outside our window. The compartment shakes. There is a great belch of acrid smoke.

211

'Off the train! Now!'

'I don't want to get off the train, Papa!' Micki cries, snuggling against me. I wrap my arms around her. If we get off the train, we'll be without protection, exposed to falling shrapnel from bombs and anti-aircraft fire.

'Everyone out!'

Another bomb explodes. The shock wave sends jagged vibrations through the floorboards. I begin praying out loud: 'Lord my God and God of the universe, Creator of all that lives, although I pray for continued life, still I know that I am mortal. Give me courage to accept whatever befalls me . . .' Some of the women join me, 'Into Your hands I commend my spirit, both when I sleep and when I wake. Body and soul are Yours, and in Your presence, Lord, I cast off fear and am at rest . . .'

A guard appears in the doorway. 'Outside!' His eyes are full of fear. 'Now!'

I lift my head as another bomb explodes. The brilliant flash frames the guard in a hellish glow. He lowers his rifle and screams, 'Get out now, or I'll shoot!'

'Oh God!' Sophie whispers, cowering.

'My wife is very weak,' I shout. 'She won't make it off the train!'

'She dies trying, or I shoot her here!' The guard lifts his rifle.

'Come on, Sophie,' I say, struggling to my feet. 'Micki, come on.' We move out of the compartment, Sophie bracing herself against me. Outside, another guard screams, 'Get down! On your bellies!' Bombs explode beyond a fence of trees, thunder and lightning. 'Cover your heads!' Screaming. Crying. I expect shrapnel to rip through the woods in a wave of death.

'Get down!' A guard yells. 'They're targeting the train.' Quivering and crying prisoners cram themselves into the trenches that line the rim of the forest. Hundreds of others, too weak to make it to the trenches, lie haphazardly on their bellies, hugging the ground, covering their heads with their hands.

'Do what they're doing,' I tell Sophie and Micki, pointing.

Another bomb explodes and Sophie falls to her knees. I feel the heat on my face. I reach down to hold her, but she's already dropping on to her stomach. Micki follows, staying close by her mother's side. Planes roar above the treetops.

I lie next to Sophie and Micki, and try to cover them as best I can with my own body. Gradually, the explosions move away to the opposite side of the woods.

It feels as if hours have pass before the world is quiet again. Thankfully, no one is hurt and the train is unharmed. The guards order everyone back on board, and we begin moving again.

Late in the afternoon of our fourth day, the train stops in the town of Ülzen. We haven't eaten in two days. After last night's bombing, everyone inside the compartment is physically and emotionally drained. Sophie moves in and out of consciousness. Two of the women cover her with their shawls to ease her fever. But I know it won't be enough to help her. She is dying. Even my prayers aren't helping. I doubt if she is strong enough to survive another air strike.

An elderly woman comes by our compartment and leaves two food parcels. They contain sugar cubes, lumps of stale bread, and sausage – a wonderful meal. Sophie rouses just long enough to eat, her eyes fluttering open and closed as she shivers. By the time we roll out of Ülzen station, she has drifted back into a ragged sleep.

That night, in the woods, just on the outskirts of Ülzen, the train stops again. The sound of footsteps on the gravel outside breaks the silence. With the click of a flashlight, a guard appears in the doorway of the compartment. 'We will stay in these woods until the next air strike is over,' he says, his chest heaving as he speaks. 'The train must remain dark or we'll be attacked.' His eyes meet mine. 'If anyone so much as lights a match, their throat will be cut before the sulphur burns away.' The flashlight clicks off, and the footsteps crunch back into the darkness.

A few hours later, bombs rain down from the sky, exploding all around the train. We huddle together, arms over our heads in a vain attempt at protection. The guards make no attempt to force us outside. Explosions rock the train and send great scars of light ripping through the woods. I feel the impacts against my chest. Micki presses against my side, too terrified to scream. Sophie cries softly, muttering words I can't understand. The air raid lasts, on and off, for over six hours. Miraculously, the train, the passengers, and the tracks have once again survived the onslaught, and we roll forward.

Late the next morning, we stop in the town of Stendhal. I step out of the compartment to stretch my legs and find the town in ruins. The ground, charred black and littered with cinders, smoulders from the devastation. I crawl back into our compartment, feeling dizzy. Even that small amount of exertion exhausts me, and I lose consciousness.

I wake up on the floor of the compartment to Micki's voice: 'Here, Papa,' she pushes a cup towards me, 'drink this.' I take the cup and drink the brown water. The morning light filters in through the window of the compartment. The train isn't moving. Either I haven't been asleep for long, or I have been out for a full day. Sophie sits slumped against the window, eyes closed.

'How's Mama?'

'Your wife is sleeping,' one of the women says. I feel disoriented, vague questions seem to come into my mind, then fade. 'You slept through the night,' the woman tells me. 'Peasants from a local village say we're close to the front lines.'

I struggle to my feet, my legs shaking. My skin feels brittle, like parchment, as if it might flake away at any moment. The walls spin, and I fight to maintain my balance as the world jerks and tumbles. My thoughts flash in jarring, fleeting images. But one thought is clear: my family is dying. The train is close to the front lines, but Sophie is close to death, Micki is frail, and my hunger is consuming me. We are all dying.

'How long have we been standing still?' I ask.

'A few hours,' the woman replies.

'Outside!' The guards shout. 'Air raid! Everyone off the train!'

Fear clears my head. If we are close to the front, the bombers will surely attack the train. A woman helps me to rouse Sophie, and we crawl out of the compartment, cowering in the ditches beside the tracks, protecting our heads with our hands.

Although the bombs land close by, the explosions sound far away. I wait for the blast of heat that will ignite the train into a fiery ball; wait for the shards of shrapnel that will shred our flesh. Distant explosions. Gunfire off through the trees. Crying. The world around me screams with the rage of fighting men.

When the bombs stop, I clamber to my feet and look around, but see no damage to the train or any of its passengers. The guards order everyone back on board. The distant sound of gunfire continues to filter through the trees.

I collapse on the floor of the compartment. If the Germans don't kill me, the bombs will, and if the bombs don't, the climbing on and off the train certainly will.

We wait for the train to move, but it stays still. There are wails from the other prisoners. I look out the window. A guard approaches, poking his head into each compartment. When he appears at our window, he says, 'The engineer stole the engine during the air raid. Wait inside until we instruct you otherwise.'

We are going no farther. I prop my back against the wall and focus all my remaining strength on clearing my head. This will be our last hurdle. The Allies are close. The guards will have to make a decision now. Will they fight, flee, or turn their guns on us?

As the sun sets on the horizon, long ribbons of artillery fire flash against the dark sky. I hold my starving daughter, watch my dying wife sleep, and listen to the Germans losing the war.

Early the next morning, the guards order a roll-call. 'Everyone off the train!'

I gather my courage. This could be it. After all our struggles, our lives might very well end here, with the Allies just over the horizon. Climbing down from the train, I step into the harsh morning sunlight. I look around. Half the guards are missing. Did they run off during the night? Or are they lying in the ditches with their guns ready for us?

On a hill to my left, I see a road. Silhouettes of men stand up there – shadows against the sun. I raise my hand to shield my eyes. They are the missing guards. But they are not in a fighting stance. Their rifles are not trained on the 2,000 or so desperate Jews down here. In fact, I can't see their rifles at all. They aren't even standing. They're sitting, each mounted on a bicycle, and balancing another bicycle next to him.

One guard climbs down the hillside near the rear of the train, very close to where I stand with my family. He immediately begins arguing with the leader. I can't hear what they're saying, but I feel the need to know. The tall shape of our elder, Aleksy Solowejczik, arrives silently at my side. We move closer to the guards.

'Our orders are clear,' the leader is saying.

'Maybe to you,' the guard replies.

'What orders?' I whisper to Solowejczik. He shrugs.

Gunfire cracks in the distance behind us.

'My orders come from Berlin!' the leader shouts.

'We'll all die if we stay here!' the younger one retaliates.

'We are to move the Jews across the Elbe River or kill them before the Allies arrive.'

My terror escalates into panic. Without an engine, the train can't possibly carry us across the river. And the Allies are so close . . .

'These Jews won't make it a kilometre on foot, much less across the river, and we can't wait any longer. If you're going to kill them, do it now and let's get out of here!'

'I don't want to kill them.'

I turn to Solowejczik. 'Go and talk to them.'

'And say what?'

'Ask them not to kill us.' I press my hand against his back and urge him forward.

He steps toward them. 'Excuse me,' he says in his perfect German, so familiar, so sudden. I believe he startled even himself. The guards' heads turn towards him, their faces knotted with rage. 'I understand your concern over your orders.' Their eyes widen. 'The war is almost over, my friends.' He speaks to them with dignity and respect as an engineer to a business associate. 'Once the war is over, the men you fear will no longer have any power over you. You will have no one to answer to, but yourselves.' Their faces slacken. Either they agree with him, or they are preparing to shoot him.

He doesn't give them time to respond, doesn't give them time to think. He opens his arms to them and starts walking, guiding them along the tracks behind the train. 'You don't have to kill anyone here. You don't have to kill anyone anymore. Leave us unharmed, and we will vouch for you. If you're captured, we will all vouch for your fairness. Imagine the weight of 2,000 people coming to your defence.'

The guards look at each other for the first time since Solowejczik approached them.

He keeps walking, keeps talking. 'I can assure you, I will not vouch for the men who forced my family into the ghettos, or those who murdered women and children. But I will vouch for you. You have treated us with as much kindness as was possible.'

The leader holds Solowejczik's gaze. The silence between them stretches and grows, then fades back into the sounds of approaching gunfire. I feel he should say more, I want him desperately to say more, but he stands there and waits, staring into the dark cold eyes of the man who holds the lives of us all in his hands. Why doesn't he say something?

'We should leave them,' the younger guard says, fidgeting.

Solowejczik doesn't look away from the leader. The leader blinks, then looks back at his captives, most of whom are sitting on the ground, lacking the strength to stay on their feet.

'The Allies are close,' Solowejczik finally says softly, convincingly. 'You have no time to worry about us.' He cocks his head: 'Listen.' The deep vibration of diesel engines rumbles through the ground. The approaching gunfire gets closer and closer.

Solowejczik smiles – a warm, caring smile: 'They're almost here. You'd better hurry.'

Fear sweeps across the leader's face. He waves to the other guards. '*Achtung!*' 'We leave now,' he calls to his men. The guards look around, bewildered. '*Schnell!*' he yells. He turns toward Solowejczik, his eyes full of terror and rage. He runs past him and scrambles up the hill to the road, small stones rattling down the slope behind him. The other guards follow, some dropping their rifles as they run. Once on the road, they climb on the extra bicycles and pedal away furiously.

I walk over to Solowejczik and we both collapse to the ground. 'You did it, my friend,' I tell him. 'You saved our lives.'

The prisoners begin to move around and, as understanding gradually takes hold, they start talking to each other and cheering. I hear the sound of Micki's voice, and I turn. She leads Sophie toward me – two walking skeletons, brittle, delicate. Sophie looks at me with recognition on her face and smiles.

I hear a loud clattering behind me. I turn and see American tanks on the road, their metal treads churning up clouds of dust. I push myself to my feet, wrap my arms around my wife and daughter, and look up at the road. The guards are nowhere in sight.

A tank stops. The muzzle of its huge gun points to where the guards fled. More cheering, loud, enthusiastic, sweeter than any symphony I can remember. Some of the passengers try to climb the hillside to greet our liberators, but they stumble and slide back.

'Is it true?' Sophie asks, her voice rough, dry: 'Are we finally free, David?'

I nod, my throat tight: 'Yes, *Häschen*, it's true. We made it.' I tighten my arms around her and Micki, and blink back tears. 'We're free.'

She lays her head on my chest and wraps her arms around my waist. 'You did it, David. Just as you promised, you got us through the war.'

I laugh. 'We wouldn't have made it without the help of many good people. But we did it. We outlived the Third Reich.'

Epilogue

Once we were well enough to travel, I took Sophie and Micki to my parents' home in Palestine. We arrived in Haifa on 23 June 1945.

We never again saw our nanny, Wanda Szcepanska, or my boss, Janina Joblanska, or Eisner's secretary, Fräulein Demske, or my smuggling partner, Rolf Schmitz, or our friends Elga and Richard Kruger, who shared their ghetto apartment with us, or Aleksy Solowejczik who convinced the train guards not to kill us. Nor have we ever heard what happened to any of them.

Sophie's niece and nephew, Halina and Staziek Walfisz, were deported from Warsaw to a labour camp in Eastern Poland where they worked until the end of the war. Halina never forgave me for not saving her mother during the factory selections, and she never spoke to me again. She stayed in Poland after the war and worked the rest of her life for the Communist Party. Staziek eventually made his way to Palestine and was reconciled with us. He spent the rest of his life in Israel.

Tragically, Sophie never recovered from all that she suffered during the war. After arriving in Palestine, she was diagnosed with chronic incurable depression. The condition worsened whenever she spent extended time with me – my presence reminding her of the terror she lived with for so long. On the advice of her doctors, we divorced in 1946. Sophie never remarried. She stayed in Israel, under doctors' care, until her death in November 1994. She was eighty-two.

At the time of our divorce, I placed Micki in a Kibbutz outside Haifa. To pay for her education, I worked two jobs. When Micki was 16, she transferred to a nursing school, completed a four-year training course, and became an X-ray nurse. She married in 1960, still lives in Israel, and has a daughter and two grandsons.

In September of 1947 – a year after my divorce – I met Liesel Hirsch, another German-born Jew. Our similar backgrounds led to romance, and we married in 1948. Our son Raphael was born in 1950.

To escape the financial hardships and political turmoil in Israel, I decided to move my new family to the United States. Before leaving, however, I was reunited with my younger brother. Peter and Eva had successfully escaped into Russia. Once there, they separated. After the war, Peter travelled to Israel to be with our family. He lived there for the rest of his life.

When we arrived in the United States in 1953, I changed our surname to Gilbert. It sounded more American. And I set out to establish myself in the business community. A year later, I became a partner in the American Bristle Company.

In 1955 Liesel gave birth to our daughter, Debbie, in New York City. Two years later, I sold my ownership in American Bristle and opened my own business importing paintbrush handles. Using the lessons I learned during the war (i.e. take action, solve problems, never give up), the Gilbert Trading Company quickly flourished.

In 1968 I fulfilled the promise I made to God while in Bergen-Belsen. I purchased a Torah and donated it to Temple Beth El in Closter, New Jersey.

In 1979 our daughter Debbie died of dysautonomia, a Jewish genetic disorder. After her death, I lost interest in my business and sold it in 1983. We retired to San Diego, California. Unable to retire completely, I joined the San Diego chapter of the

Service Corps of Retired Executives Association and engaged in public speaking about my wartime experiences.

Liesel and I celebrated our fiftieth wedding anniversary in 1998. The following year, we sold our home in San Diego and moved to Walnut Creek in northern California so we could be closer to our son Raphael, and our three granddaughters.

Every year, up until Sophie's death in 1994, Liesel and I travelled to Israel to visit her. Between visits, we spoke with her regularly by phone.